CONSULTANT–
MARKET
YOURSELF

Raise Your Profile and Attract New Business

Robert Gentle

KOGAN
PAGE

This book has been endorsed by the Institute of Directors.

The endorsement is given to selected Kogan Page books which the IoD recognizes as being of specific interest to its members and providing them with up-to-date, informative and practical resources for creating business success. Kogan Page books endorsed by the IoD represent the most authoritative guidance available on a wide range of subjects including management, finance, marketing, training and HR.

The views expressed in this book are those of the author and are not necessarily the same as those of the Institute of Directors

First published in 2002

Kogan Page Limited
120 Pentonville Road
London N1 9JN
UK

Kogan Page US
22 Broad Street
Milford CT 06460
USA

British Library Cataloguing in Publication Data

A CIP record for this book is available from the British Library.

ISBN 0 7494 3693 X

Typeset by Jean Cussons Typesetting, Diss, Norfolk
Printed and bound in Great Britain by Clays Ltd, St Ives plc

Contents

Doing business without advertising is like winking at a girl in the dark: you know what you are doing, but nobody else does.

Edgar Watson Howe
(quoted in Metcalf, 1986: 11)

Introduction

Marketing takes place <u>before</u> you meet the client, otherwise you face an uphill battle getting new business.

There are three ways you can get business as a consultant:

- You to client: 'Can I do some work for you?'
- You to client: 'I'm really good. Can I do some work for you?'
- Client to you: 'We've heard you're really good, and we'd like you to do some work for us.'

It's the third option that you're going to learn about in this book. The first two are little more than crude hawking, and are almost always ineffectual. When you meet a potential client for the first time, that client should already have heard about you, otherwise you face an uphill battle.

The point is neatly illustrated in an old but memorable advertisement, which shows a stern executive sitting in a swivel chair. He is addressing a salesman – but he could just as well be addressing a consultant like yourself. Here's what he says:

I don't know who you are.
I don't know your company.
I don't know your company's product.
I don't know what your company stands for.
I don't know your company's customers.
I don't know your company's reputation.
Now – what was it you wanted to sell me?

an old advertisement for McGraw-Hill Magazines
(quoted in Ogilvy, 1983: 118)

This superb speech shows the pitfalls of doing business in a vacuum. So does the foregoing quote about winking in the dark. However, they are both misleading because they suggest – perhaps self-servingly – that advertising is the only way to build awareness.

It isn't – not by a long shot. Welcome to the world of multidimensional marketing, where different media – from flyers and mailshots to media articles and lectures – combine to help build your public profile.

There is no bad publicity, except an obituary notice.

Brendan Behan
(quoted in MacHale, 1996: 141)

1

What is a public profile?

It is all the sensory impressions that the market has about you
and your business.

Tony Blair's got one. Tiger Woods has got one. Pamela Anderson
has certainly got one! But you, a 'mere' corporate consultant: can
you have a public profile, too? You bet. After all, a public profile is
essentially the sum total of all the sensory impressions that people
in the market receive of you and your business. Advertising is one
such sensory impression; media coverage is another. But there are
many others.

To illustrate this, let's examine the public profile of a well-known
corporate entity like, say, Coca-Cola. How do we perceive such a
company? Well, let us count the ways:

- telephone directory (print and electronic);
- Coca-Cola Web site;
- other Web sites;
- TV advertisements;
- outdoor billboards;
- trade and industry directories (print and electronic);
- pamphlets, posters;

- radio reports;
- newspaper articles;
- radio advertisements;
- magazine articles;
- conference speeches;
- TV news reports;
- mailshots;
- movies;
- TV shows;
- collectables fairs;
- published studies on the soft-drink industry;
- published studies on Coca-Cola;
- annual report to shareholders;
- a presentation to investors;
- personal friendship with a Coca-Cola employee;
- a book about the soft-drink industry;
- drinking a Coke.

It is each of these sensory impressions, however small or insignificant, that contributes to Coca-Cola's public profile – some would say brand or brand image.

THE SEVEN ELEMENTS OF A PUBLIC PROFILE

At first glance, the list of sensory impressions seems to be a rather jumbled mess. On closer inspection, however, it turns out that there is a clear order and pattern to it. All the important items fit into seven neat categories:

- directory listings;
- advertising;
- media coverage;
- lectures and speeches;
- published studies;

The greatest risk of all is the risk of going unnoticed.

Bill Bernbach
(quoted in Ehrlich, 1998)

- newsletters;
- books.

Suddenly, the creation of a public profile seems a lot less myste-rious. Clearly, there's nothing random about it: if you do certain things, your consultancy will acquire a public profile. If you don't, you run the risk of going unnoticed. It's that simple. What's less simple, however, is knowing how to exploit each of these cat–egories.

RELATIVE IMPORTANCE OF EACH ELEMENT

The seven categories of sensory impressions are not equal; each operates in very specific ways. For example, blanket advertising may work wonders for certain kinds of companies, but achieve precious little for others. Here are just some of the factors that influ-ence this:

- Do you sell a product or a service? (You don't promote apples in the same way as, say, investment services.)
- How big is your target market? (Advertising tends to work well for large markets rather than small ones.)
- Can you identify and locate each customer? (If you can, you could reach them directly using mailshots or newsletters.)
- Is your product or service difficult or easy to understand? (Pension plans need lengthy explanations; a soft drink doesn't.)
- Is your product or service a one-off, or can customers keep on using it? (Repeat business implies the need for ongoing commu-nication.)
- Is there a lot of competition? (The more captive your market, the less you have to market yourself.)

It comes as no surprise that companies that sell mass-market products (eg clothes, beer) to a largely anonymous market tend

Some entrepreneurs see advertising as the solution to the problem of getting into prospects' minds. Advertising isn't cheap. It cost $9,000 a minute to fight World War II. It cost $22,000 a minute to fight the Vietnam war. A one-minute commercial on the NFL Super Bowl will cost you almost $2 million.

Jack Trout with Steve Rivkin
(Trout, 2000)

to advertise a lot. On the other hand, they are unlikely to send regular newsletters or product updates to their customers – especially as it would be well-nigh impossible to track them down. At the other end of the spectrum, companies that sell specialized services such as personal investment or legal services will, in addition to advertising, have to promote themselves heavily in the business media, speak at conferences and send regular updates to key clients. Needless to say, consultancy falls into this category.

EACH ELEMENT OF THE PROFILE IS FUNDAMENTALLY DIFFERENT

You may have figured out by now that each of our seven activities requires a different degree of intellectual effort. For example, while it will take you only a few minutes to get your company listed in the local telephone directory, it will take you days – if not weeks – to conduct market research on trends in your industry sector, write up a report and send it to potential clients.

Figure 1.1 shows how the seven activities stack up in terms of time and effort.

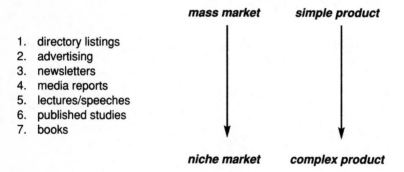

1. directory listings
2. advertising
3. newsletters
4. media reports
5. lectures/speeches
6. published studies
7. books

Figure 1.1 *The marketing approach for complex or niche businesses (eg consultancy) requires greater intellectual depth*

What this figure shows is that if your product or service is simple and aimed at a mass market, your public profile is likely to result from simple activities such as directory listings and basic advertising. On the other hand, the more your product or service is complex and aimed at a niche market, the more your public profile is likely to result from more complex activities, eg media reports, lectures, published studies and books. Again, consultancy fits into the latter category.

This doesn't mean that simple concept/mass-market companies must avoid lectures, published studies or books; or that complex concept/niche-market companies must never use simple publicity methods such as directory listings or advertising. However, as we see below, the relative emphasis on each of the seven activities will be different, as will be their relative effectiveness (see Figure 1.2).

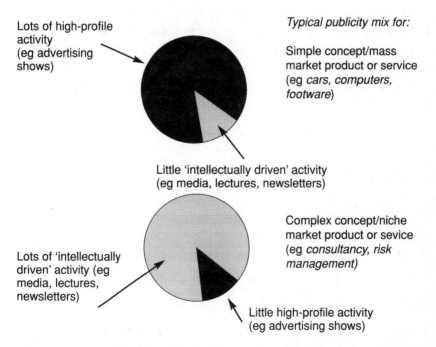

Figure 1.2 *Typical publicity mix for simple versus complex products/services*

Anita Roddick built the Body Shop into a major brand with no advertising. Instead she travelled the world on a relentless quest for publicity, pushing her ideas about the environment. It was the endless torrent of newspaper and magazine articles, plus radio and television interviews, that literally created the Body Shop brand.

Al Ries and Laura Ries
(1998)

EACH ELEMENT INFLUENCES ALL THE OTHERS

A public profile is a multifaceted, multidimensional affair. Each element of the mix reinforces the others to produce an overall sensory impression in the marketplace. Your directory listings remind people of your advertisements; your advertisements remind people of your media coverage; your media coverage reminds people of your newsletters – and so on. This results in a virtuous circle (see Figure 1.3).

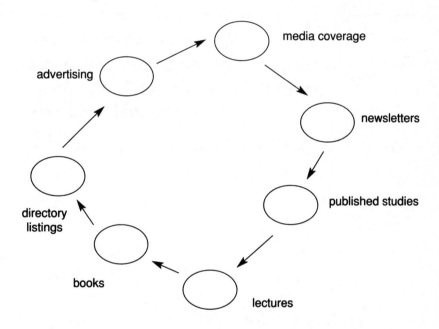

Figure 1.3 *The seven publicity activities reinforce one another to form a virtuous circle*

The lines between advertising, media and content are blurring. A branding idea can start on any platform, then cross over to others to create a total brand experience.

Keith Reinhard
Chairman, DDB Worldwide
(quoted in Financial Mail, *South Africa, 25 May 2001)*

In reality, the figure is a lot more complex because each element influences not just the one next to it, but all the others as well, often at the same time and in unexpected ways. For example, during the mid-1990s, the wine sector suddenly received a major publicity boost after a scientific study concluded that red wine reduces certain forms of cholesterol, and that a glass or two per day might actually be good for one's health. The news was picked up in the media, resulted in more studies, prompted lectures, produced innovative advertising and was mentioned in several books on health and nutrition.

Without the considerable effect of this publicity, the study would not have had the impact that it did on the public profile of the wine industry. (Of course, as often happens in the area of health and nutrition, another study might well appear in the future claiming to prove the opposite – but that's another story.) Either way, it illustrates the importance of not confining oneself to just one medium when building a public profile.

FINALLY, DON'T FORGET DELIVERY

Building a public profile is one thing, but maintaining it is something else – and that can only rest on a foundation of delivery. In other words, your product or service had better meet – or exceed – the expectations of your target market. You have to deliver what your public profile suggests you are capable of delivering, otherwise word of mouth will kill you, no matter how often you advertise, appear in the media or have books written about you. If the delivery is not consistent with the promise, you're dead in the water. Abraham Lincoln was right when he said that you can fool all of the people some of the time, and some of the people all of the time – but you can't fool all of the people all of the time.

Welcome to [insert your favourite phone company here]. We value your call. You are number 257 in the queue, and it will take approximately 28 minutes for your call to be answered [irritating music follows].

Anonymous

2

Get listed in national directories

Make sure you're in the phone book and other directories –
otherwise people may not know where to reach you.

OFTEN OVERLOOKED – THE PHONE BOOK

It's amazing how many consultants – this author included – get so carried away with producing business cards and corporate brochures when they get started that they overlook the most obvious promotional tool – the telephone directory.

If you aren't already listed, contact your telephone company now and give them your address details for the next issue of the directory. If you miss the publication deadline, you may have to wait as much as 12 months. A week is a long time in politics, but a year is an eternity in business.

DON'T FORGET DIRECTORY ENQUIRIES

Perhaps more important than the physical phone book in today's electronic age is the electronic phone book – or directory enquiries.

That's simply a number one rings (eg 192 in the UK) to speak to a telephone operator who gives out the contact details of most businesses and organizations. If you aren't on the system, contact your local telephone company and give them your details. A word of advice: call directory enquiries a few days later, pretend to be a potential customer and check to see if the information given out is correct. Mistakes happen.

GET INTO TRADE AND BUSINESS DIRECTORIES

The most valuable directories in which to list your business are the numerous business reference books issued by:

- trade organizations;
- umbrella bodies;
- industry associations;
- local government bodies;
- government departments;
- industry magazines;
- business newspapers.

No matter what sector you consult in, you should be able to identify at least half a dozen such directories. Some of them are so thick that they could easily double as a doorstop or, if dropped from a great enough height, a lethal weapon. However, never judge a directory by its size, but rather by its content, readership and method of distribution. Some directories are professionally put together by reputable publishing houses and very accurately targeted; buying space in them is usually well worth the investment. Other directories are shoddily designed and poorly distributed, and are often nothing more than moneymaking schemes.

A magnum opus is a book which when dropped from a three-storey building is big enough to kill a man.

Edward Wilson
(quoted in MacHale, 1997: 55)

You'll find that as your consultancy business becomes better known, these publishers will phone you at least once a year and give you a smooth sales pitch about how your business will be on the lips of every CEO in the land if only you buy some space in their directories. Hear them out – then check them out. Here are some obvious questions to ask:

- What distinguishes your directory from those of your competitors?
- How many editions have you printed so far?
- Are your directories sold or given away?
- In how many different ways can information in the directory be accessed, besides alphabetically?
- Have you ever polled your readers on their actual use of the directory?
- What percentage of companies listed in last year's directory have elected to buy space again this year?
- Do you have an online version too?
- What organizations, if any, have endorsed your directory?
- How often is your directory updated – quarterly, six-monthly or annually?

The last point is particularly important because directories are only as accurate as the information in them. For example, if you know you're likely to change premises in the next six months, avoid directories that are updated annually.

THE DOWNSIDE OF DIRECTORIES

You should regard directories as a back-up source of factual information on your company rather than as the primary means for potential clients to seek you out. After all, people are more likely to choose a consultant they've already heard of than look one up cold in the directory the way you look up an emergency glass repairer if your window is suddenly broken. Being listed in a directory is the very least you can do as a business; but understand that it's merely a way of telling the market that your company exists. What directories don't do very well is provide a persuasive reason for people to use you in the first place.

You cannot hope to bribe or twist,
Thank God! the British journalist.
But seeing what the man will do
Unbribed, there's no occasion to.

Humbert Wolfe
(quoted in Metcalf, 1986: 141)

3

Get into the media

This is where you show the world just how good you are in your area of expertise.

There may be no such thing as a free lunch, but there is such a thing as free publicity, and as a consultant you are probably better placed than anyone to get it.

Why? Because, like all good consultants, you've developed a high – if not exaggerated – level of expertise in a given subject, whether it's computers, human resources, emotional intelligence or any of the dozens of areas of specialization in today's modern business world. After all, that's why you became a consultant in the first place.

That expertise is your trump card. If there were quiz shows on your subject, you'd probably win hands down. But there aren't, so you need another platform on which to shine, and that platform is the opinion pages of major newspapers and magazines. And by major, we're talking serious middleweight and heavyweight publications, not suburban free-sheets. Whether you live in New York, London or Johannesburg, there are countless such publications:

- business dailies, eg *The Wall Street Journal, Financial Times, Business Day*;
- news dailies, eg *The New York Times, The Daily Telegraph, The Star*;

- business weeklies, eg *Fortune, Eurobusiness, Financial Mail*;
- specialist and trade publications, eg *Inc, Campaign, Computer Week*;
- general interest publications, eg *The New Yorker, GQ, Style*.

WHAT DOES IT TAKE TO GET COVERAGE?

You're probably thinking that you'll never get a quote in any of these publications, never mind an entire article! Well, don't you believe it. Getting published is not that hard if you go about it properly. It's less about good writing ability and more about attitude, confidence and the willingness to stick your neck out. Here are the four key attributes you need if you want to get published:

- **An insatiable, wide-ranging curiosity.** You should be reading at least two newspapers a day and flipping through a dozen or so magazines a week, even if they're not all on your subscription list. These days, you can go into your local bookshop, grab a cappuccino and while away 40 minutes flipping through everything from *GQ* and *Flight International* to the *Spectator* and the *New Yorker*. Don't neglect books: if you aren't reading at least one non-fiction book a month, then you're not plugged in to what's happening in the world.
- **The ability to see the bigger picture.** News doesn't exist in a vacuum; everything is connected. All newspapers and publications, from the *Washington Post* to *Cosmopolitan*, tackle the same fundamental issues, but from specific angles that appeal to their readership. For example, the story in a heavyweight financial daily on the emigration of top-level IT specialists to the United States may crop up in a different guise in other publications. A property magazine may do a feature on the glut of luxury homes that have come on to the market as a result; or a women's weekly may look at how families cope with selling up, moving abroad and settling

The paper had over a million readers, many of whom could read.

Louella Parsons
(quoted in Jarski, 2000: 192)

into another culture. If you're quick to spot these connections, you can come up with many interesting and topical story ideas.

- **The willingness to articulate your own point of view.** Having a view on a given issue is one thing; having the courage to make that view public is another. When you're a consultant, that courage should be second nature. After all, it's not as if you work for a big organization that might fire you for articulating a view that is at odds with company policy. You're your own boss. Companies hire you for your views and advice. Having the courage of your convictions is great for business because it brings those views to the attention of potential clients.

- **The ability to produce short, persuasive copy.** What do your letters, reports and proposals say about you as a writer? Are you liked and respected for getting to the point using short sentences and plain English? Or are you notorious for rambling, long-winded prose and a penchant for pretentious words (such as 'penchant')? Newspapers and magazines like simplicity, brevity and a straightforward argument that's easy to follow. So learn to write in a top-down manner (ie make your point at the beginning, not the end); use plain, conversational English; and make your copy come alive with interesting anecdotes, observations and analogies. And if you can get away with being amusing or witty, go for it.

This may seem like a tall order, but it isn't. It's the kind of writing you used to do at school before your university lecturers got hold of you and conned you into believing that obfuscation and pretentiousness were worthy goals. If you know which publications you want to write for, then you already have a good idea of the writing style you should be adopting. Practice makes perfect: your third piece will be far better than your first and second. The thing is to start.

Literature is the art of writing something that will be read twice; journalism what will be read once.

*Cyril Connolly
(quoted in Ratcliffe, 2000)*

WHAT KIND OF ARTICLES SHOULD YOU BE WRITING?

Open a newspaper or magazine and see if you can categorize the various articles. You'll find there are four broad types of coverage:

- news stories (man bites dog);
- editorial pieces (dogs should be kept on leashes);
- opinion pieces by outsiders (having a dog is a constitutional right);
- letters to the editor (this is an insult to dogs everywhere).

Let's look at these in more detail.

News stories

This is the everyday stuff that is topical, newsworthy and important. It includes everything from births and deaths to the latest medical breakthrough or hostile corporate takeover. It's relatively difficult for you to crack this category, as virtually nothing that happens in your small company from day to day – not even the signing of a major new client – is likely to be of the slightest interest to Joe and Jane Reader. However, if you are well known, the newspaper may well ask you for your opinion on a new development related to your area of expertise.

Editorial pieces

This is what you usually find on the editorial page towards the middle, where the editor and various senior columnists hold forth on issues of the day. By definition, this is off limits to anyone who doesn't work for the publication.

Opinion pieces by outsiders

This is the main area where you, the consultant, can score. Most commercial publications welcome articles by outsiders who, by virtue of their expertise or position of authority, are qualified to write a column on a given subject. The more interesting, topical and suitably controversial the topic, the more likely it is to appeal to the editors. For example, the likelihood of getting brain cancer from using a cellphone was once a hot topic; now it's old hat unless you can find an interesting new angle. However, it's not a case of anything goes: magazines publish for their readership. A virulently anti-business piece attacking the merits of free trade is unlikely to be accepted by the *Financial Times* – and would in any case not impress your potential clients unless they happened to be radical, left-wing trade unionists.

Letters to the editor

This is another area where you, as consultant, can get a free plug. Who you are matters a lot less to the newspaper than whether your letter makes an interesting point. Contrary views are actively courted, even those that attack the publication on a given issue. Beware of verbosity, though: the ability to put an argument across in a couple of tight paragraphs – 100 to 300 words – is more critical here than in any other kind of writing. The shorter the letter, the more likely it is to be published. Letter columns are widely read, and a published letter with your name, company and e-mail address clearly mentioned is worth its weight in gold. Finally, be prepared to be attacked by other readers who might not agree with your views. That said, resist the temptation to respond, unless you're the subject of defamation. There's nothing that bores readers more than a pair of egotistical correspondents engaged in a slanging match. Just let it go. Letter columns are for people with thick skins. If you can't stand the heat...

I've always said there's a place for the press, but they haven't dug it yet.

Tommy Docherty
(quoted in MacHale, 1997: 114)

Checklist

Dos and don'ts about letters to the editor

- Keep them short and tight.

- Write while the issue is topical – otherwise it goes cold.

- If readers counter-attack in letters of their own, don't respond – just let it go.

- Be firm and forthright, but avoid a know-it-all tone – no one likes a smart alec.

- Don't become a fixture on letters pages – once a month is more than enough.

HOW TO SPOT A STORY OPPORTUNITY

Story opportunities will fall into your lap if you keep an open mind. More often than not, ideas will strike while you're going through your daily newspaper at your desk, flipping through a magazine over lunch or listening to the radio in your car on your way to a meeting. If you get excited or angry about an issue, that's a good sign: you can use that energy to fire off a quick e-mail to the letters page, or do a more considered opinion piece. Some examples are given in Table 3.1.

An idea may hit you when you least expect it. For example, if you're an architectural consultant, you may have noticed that every second pillar in underground car parks has black scrape marks on it from some car having brushed up against it. There can't be that many lousy drivers around, so it's probably because of bad design. Why can't they place the parking bays at an angle for easier access instead of always putting them at right angles, which makes for awkward head-turning and limited visibility? Now there's an interesting piece, trivial though it may be in the overall scheme of things.

Table 3.1 *What you could write about*

You're a consultant in	You read or hear about	You could write an opinion piece or letter on
verbal communication	telesales representatives from disadvantaged backgrounds saying potential customers discriminate against them on the phone	the psychology of voice and accent, and how these colour people's perception of you – particularly when they can't see you
commercial floor planning and design	pandemonium and overcrowding in a major store as a result of a special promotion that attracts hordes of people	the importance of wider aisles and extra cash registers when traffic flow through the store exceeds a critical level
Web site design	statistics showing that many Web site visitors quit in frustration because they can't find what they're looking for	the importance of testing Web sites before they go live, using real users

HOW SHOULD YOU APPROACH A PUBLICATION?

Getting into the media is a Nike thing – just do it. If it's a letter to the editor, write it as quickly as possible and fire it off by e-mail or fax. Avoid the post – it takes too long. When you sign it, remember to include your job title, for example John Smith, Chief Executive, The Change Management Consultancy, London. Add your e-mail address and Web site too; some publications include them in your address.

The secret of successful journalism is to make your readers so angry that they are ready to write half your paper for you.

C E M Joad
(quoted in Lamb, 2000)

If it's an article you've written, don't waste your time asking the publication for permission first; by the time an answer comes back – if indeed it ever does – the window of opportunity may have closed. If you know that the publication accepts articles from outsiders, just sit down, open a fresh file on your PC and write the thing. Then send it off by e-mail. Don't bother with faxing or using the postal service; they're far too slow in today's fast-moving world of daily and weekly deadlines. If you haven't heard from them within 10 days, chances are your article hasn't made it. Don't get angry; rather e-mail them back saying thanks for taking the time to consider the article. Then propose it to some other publication. Statistically, you will have articles rejected from time to time; it comes with the territory. To maximize your chances of publication, keep your articles fresh and topical. And a bit of controversy won't hurt either.

Don't ask for money, even though some publications do offer payment. Remember that this is an investment in your career. Your pay-off will come in the form of a heightened public profile. Eventually, as you become better known, newspapers and magazines may ask you to write a piece for them – and they'll pay you for it too. Then you'll know you've arrived!

| **Checklist** |

Dos and don'ts in dealing with editors

- Don't keep phoning to find out when your article is going to be used.

- Don't worry about why a given article hasn't appeared yet; start working on the next one.

- Don't quibble about routine changes to your article; editors usually have a better nose for what needs to be cut than you.

The Ten Commandments

The Sun
Ten things you never knew you shouldn't do

The Express *(sports page)*
Moses names ten for Sunday

The Times
Graven image manufacturers protest at new guidelines

(BBC, 1998)

- Don't insist on a published correction to any of your articles except in extreme circumstances; be thankful that you got it published at all.

- If an article is rejected, accept that there was a good reason for it – and move on to the next one.

WHAT ABOUT RADIO AND TV?

Because there are comparatively fewer radio and TV stations than newspapers and magazines, getting into these audio-visual media is a lot harder. The process is the same – but you have to keep whatever you send them a lot shorter because airtime is always limited. Radio is the better bet, and you'll find that as your press profile grows, so does the likelihood that a radio reporter will call you and ask to interview you – usually by phone during a news programme. My first ever radio interview took place after I'd written a letter to the editor of a business newspaper suggesting that the country's vice-president simplify his speeches because they were too long-winded; that very day, the host of the evening news gave me a three-minute interview on the subject.

Checklist

Dos and don'ts about radio and TV

- With barely three to five minutes of interview time, you'll never be able to say everything – so focus on just a few key points.

- Speak in soundbites that contain a single thought.

- Avoid long, rambling responses that don't make an obvious point.
- Always be polite, even when answering a difficult question.

The 'five Ws' young reporters need to know before they write their stories are Who? What? Where? When? and Why?

[In a satirical twist on this, a TV sketch for Spitting Image showed three journalists having a merry old time, shouting:] 'Whose round is it? What are we havin'? Where's the pub? When's it open? and Why don't we have another one?'

Anonymous
(quoted in Glover, 1999)

- Remember to mention your company name at least once ('At XYZ Consulting, we believe that…').

EXAMPLES OF MEDIA COVERAGE

Here are some examples of press coverage I got as a plain-language consultant specializing in rewriting complex corporate documentation and teaching executives how to write clearly.

Notice how the same theme crops up again and again, though each time with a fresh and topical angle. The constant reference to the author might appear monotonous, but it is oh so valuable in terms of brand awareness. Picture your own name there and you'll quickly appreciate this.

Letters to the editor
- Plain talk will help people to understand business
  Business Day, February 1998
  Robert Gentle, MD: Plain Business Writing
- Better annual reports
  Financial Mail, May 1998
  Robert Gentle, MD: Plain Business Writing
- Plain language a business tool
  Business Day, June 1998
  Robert Gentle, MD: Plain Business Writing
- American English has enriched 'traditional' language
  Business Day, August 1998
  Robert Gentle, MD: Plain Business Writing
- Judge to the rescue
  Financial Mail, June 2000
  Robert Gentle, MD: Plain Business Writing

We're supposed to tell stories in 30 or 35 seconds on the radio, in a minute or 90 seconds on television. That forces us to be ruthless in our selection of facts... Rather than saying 'Winds are blowing at 100 miles-an-hour and two inches of rain have fallen,' we say, 'There's a powerful storm out there.'

Brad Kalbfeld
(quoted in Associated Press, 2001)

Checklist

Three steps to a good letter

- A bold, no-nonsense first paragraph that launches straight into the point you're trying to make.

- A good supporting argument that shores up your first paragraph, preferably with humour or interesting illustrations.

- An appropriate wrap-up that drives the point home.

Here are a couple of examples of letters to the editor

Business Day, 19 August 1998

American English has enriched 'traditional' language

Sir

Bravo for daring to destroy the myth that American English, despite having strayed somewhat from the grammatical straight and narrow, is somehow sub-standard (Americans say it in neon lights, *After Hours*, 31 July).

In fact, stripped of airs and graces and rooted in the reality of everyday life, American English has enriched 'traditional' English for over 200 years. It has given us wonderfully evocative expressions (eg, *to have an axe to grind, to be on the right track, to have a chip on one's shoulder*); deadly accurate descriptions of people (eg, *con man, underdog, deadbeat*); and a string of colourful words (eg, *phoney, bogus, bamboozle*).

Language is the ultimate free market – if there's demand for a word or expression, it becomes common currency. Purists may not like it, but that's just the way it is. Or, to use an Americanism, *that's just the way the cookie crumbles*.

Robert Gentle
Managing Director
Plain Business Writing

Financial Mail, 23 June 2000

Judge to the rescue

Sir

Hooray for the court that ruled against car rental company Avis for using small print and legalese to slip a contentious clause past a customer (*Personal Wealth Weekly*, June 16). This is not the first time judges have sided with consumers in this way.

An article by Peter Butt in the November 1999 *Australian Law Journal* cites a 1983 English case, *Socpen Trustees v. Wood Nash & Winters*, in which a client successfully sued lawyers for negligence for providing a letter of advice drafted in traditional legalese. The client misunderstood its message and acted on that misunderstanding, incurring loss. The judge awarded damages of £95,000, saying that the letter 'was very obscure English' and 'anaesthetized [the client] into oblivion'.

It's all about transparency. Companies can put all the sly clauses they want into their contracts, so long as they are written in plain English and properly flagged so we can't miss them.

Ironically, had Avis come right out with a bold, upfront headline saying *'We aren't liable for damage even if it's our fault'*, it might well have won the case. Then again, it might not have succeeded in renting the car – but hey, that's consumer choice!

Robert Gentle
Managing Director
Plain Business Writing

Opinion pieces
Note the variety of publications in the following list; they come from South Africa, the UK and the USA, and range from business dailies and weeklies to specialist trade monthlies:

- Directors must start to speak plain English: competition, fuller disclosure and rising consumer expectations are changing the way companies communicate

The hardest-worked word in my vocabulary was 'alleged'. It can steer you through a mile of rapids.

R F Delderfield
(quoted in Lamb, 2000)

Directorship (quarterly magazine of the Institute of Directors), June 1998
Robert Gentle, MD: Plain Business Writing

- Poor writing plagues 90% of annual reports
  PR & Communications, September 1998
  Robert Gentle, MD: Plain Business Writing
- Plain English takes off in the South African corporate sector
  Campaign International (UK), Spring 1999
  Robert Gentle, MD: Plain Business Writing
- Findings of a study into the readability of shareholder documents
  In Brief (journal of the US Legal Secretaries Association), April 2000
  Robert Gentle, CEO: Plain Business Writing
- The human factor in business communication: or why a lot of what you write is likely to be ignored
  Executive Business Brief, October 2000
  Robert Gentle, MD: Plain Business Writing

Checklist

Three steps to a good opinion piece *

- A bold, no-nonsense first paragraph that launches straight into the point you're trying to make.

- A good supporting argument that shores up your first paragraph, preferably with humour or interesting illustrations.

- An appropriate wrap-up that drives the point home.

* Surprise, surprise! It's the same as for a good letter – the only difference is you have more space.

Here are a couple of examples of opinion pieces.

PR & Communications, September 1998

Poor writing plagues 90% of annual reports
Robert Gentle, MD Plain Business Writing

Over 90% of annual reports are so badly written that they fail basic standards of clarity, according to a study by Plain Business Writing. They feature verbose language, poor layout, no descriptive headlines and no up-front summaries at the start of key sections.

The net result is that the annual reports force the reader to wade through acres of dense, convoluted, jargon-ridden language to glimpse some sort of meaning. In the real world, however, readers have neither the time nor the inclination to do this. Consequently, they switch off after skimming a few pages.

This might seem like a harsh judgement, but it is backed up by repeated international investor research, which shows that the average shareholder reads an annual report for 3 to 5 minutes.

In the Plain Business Writing study, we randomly chose 54 annual reports issued during 1997 by various JSE-listed companies. We judged clarity, not content. Each annual report was read for 5 to 8 minutes and rated for the presence of:

1. Up-front summaries at the start of key sections to set the tone.

2. Descriptive headlines to pull the reader through.

3. A clean, airy layout to make the text stand out.

4. Short, active sentences containing plain words.

The extent to which the annual reports satisfied each of these criteria was rated on a scale of 1 to 5 as follows: 1 poor; 2 bad; 3 average; 4 good; 5 excellent.

City Lodge and Sweets from Heaven obtained the highest average score (3.25) across all categories. Investec and Perskor got the lowest average score (1) across all categories.

Even allowing for the inevitable margin of error and the fact that some companies may have been rated unfairly, the fact remains that clear, well-presented writing was the exception. A similar study on a larger sample of JSE annual reports will almost certainly produce a similar result.

We identified several other factors that got in the way of clarity:

1. Excessive use of jargon and specialist industry terms (eg, PBT for profit before tax).

2. Text which, instead of adding value, contains needless verbalisation of figures that are already apparent from tables and graphs.

3. Erudite quotations from historical personalities that bear little or no relation to the surrounding text.

4. Stunningly creative artwork that overwhelms rather than supports the text.

5. Pie charts that use colour-coded legends that are difficult to discern.

6. No numbers or headlines in the body of graphs, an omission which makes them difficult to read.

It's a safe bet that most of the R60m or so spent by JSE companies every year on annual reports is wasted because they don't communicate effectively. [Over 600 JSE companies produce annual reports that cost at least R100,000 per run, ie a total cost of R60m. That doesn't include distribution.]

Many companies think that their annual reports are effective because they disclose pertinent information. Actually, it's how that disclosure is made that's the key – otherwise it's merely disclosure for the sake of compliance.

This tendency is unwittingly encouraged by awards that test the *presence* of disclosure rather than the *effectiveness* of that disclosure. Worse, annual reports are often tested in artificial conditions (judges painstakingly read much of the document) whereas in the real world, most readers will skip right past poorly presented material.

In the US, for example, an annual report survey by investor relations firm Rein Nomm & Associates found that most readers skim though the chairman's statement because it is often written in passive and verbose language.

An example of this is the following tortuous, 80-word sentence from the first page of Alpha's 1997 annual report:

'Operating profit was adversely impacted by high operating costs mainly due to above-inflation increases in the cost of fuel, promotional and advertising cost increases relating to the Cement Division product launch, bad debt write-offs, a higher cementitious content in ready-mixed concrete dictated by market demand, lower utilisation of the ready-mixed concrete fleet and once-off costs associated with the rationalisation of certain operations and management structures in the Stone and Readymix Division in Gauteng, and customer service improvement strategies.'

The report contains many similar sentences, made all the more unreadable by a small font and a dense, wordy layout. Nevertheless, the report won 1st prize in the *Financial Mail's* annual report award.

Clearly, publications and companies that sponsor annual report awards ought to include basic clarity standards in their judging criteria. As for companies themselves, they need to start researching the impact of their annual reports by polling a sample of readers; the results may astound them.

Executive Business Brief, October 2000

The human factor in business communication: or why a lot of what you write is likely to be ignored

Robert Gentle

In the movie *Field of Dreams*, Kevin Costner is told to build a baseball field on his property by a voice which says: 'If you build it, they will come.' Executives are victims of a similar syndrome: 'If you write it, they will read.'

The mere fact of having written something – be it a letter, a report or a business plan – does NOT mean it will be read. Why? Because of several human factors which make ignoring a document altogether a relatively attractive proposition:

- **Do I have the time?**
  Information overload has reached such proportions that it's no longer a question of whether we don't read certain business documents, but how many of them we don't read. For some, reading time has come down to seconds for the trivial stuff and a couple of minutes for the serious stuff.

- **Is it interesting?**
  Unlike literature or our favourite magazine, business writing is not something we read out of interest; if that were the case, we'd all be devouring memos on holiday. Business writing is something we *have* to read in order to do our jobs; it is functional.

- **Is it urgent?**
  Information overload implies the need for time management, which in turn implies the need to prioritize. What's urgent tends to get our attention first.

- **Does it require action?**
  Are you required to do something as a result of this document? Or are you just being copied on it?

- **Do I know who wrote this?**
  A memo from John Smith whom you know will at least get a cursory glance; the same cannot always be said of a memo from someone you've never heard of.

- **Is this relevant?**
  Does the subject matter concern you? Are you the right person to be reading this? Even if it's not interesting, you might be persuaded to read it if it was relevant.

- **Is it easy to read?**
  What is the gist of this document? Is the point obvious at a glance? Most important of all, is it written in plain English?

- **Is the message available somewhere else?**
  If you're able to find the same material somewhere else – eg, on the Internet, during your next meeting or by someone calling you back – that's one more reason for you not to read it.

- **What will happen if I don't read it?**
  If you don't read it, you won't get fired – no one ever got fired for not reading a business document. At worst, you miss out on a potential business opportunity, or another banquet you didn't really want to attend in the first place.

You can never eliminate these human factors, but you can minimize their effects. So next time you sit down to write a business document, first ask yourself whether it is even necessary. Then, if it is, do your reader a favour by making it easy to read:

- keep it short

- use plain words and short, punchy sentences

- make your point up-front

- use descriptive headlines (they make the document easy to take in at a glance)

- have a clean, uncluttered layout.

And when you send your document off, time it properly – not too early or too late. You may even want to alert the recipient – especially if you don't know him – that the document is on its way.

And even then, despite all these precautions, you may still score a big, fat zero. Why? For reasons you won't even begin to fathom. That's human nature!

Gentle is author of the best-selling Plain Business Writing Series *and MD of the Johannesburg consultancy* Plain Business Writing.
Note: This article also formed the basis of a full conference talk (see page 108), which goes to show how the same idea can be exploited in many different ways.

Articles written by journalists

The higher your profile in the press, the more likely it is that journalists will mention you and/or your company in their own articles. Here is a variety of such pieces that I was fortunate enough to have written about my consultancy and its work in the field of plain language:

- Gentle persuasion: the need for reform of legal documents
  Insurance & Investments, May 1998
- Clear as fine-grained deposits, that is, mud
  Financial Mail, May 1998
- Plain English revolution sweeping business world
  Guardrisk Update, April 1999
- My word, that makes sense
  Daily News, May 1999
- Deciphering the gobbledegook
  Financial Mail, December 1999

| **Checklist** |

Three steps to a good article about your company

- See the story from the newspaper's perspective, not that of your company – that way, you'll know what kind of quotes and information to provide.

- Accept that the journalist will write the story his way: invariably, you will be part of the story, not the story itself.

- Don't ask to see the article before it runs unless the journalist offers – learn to trust the journalist's ability to get it right (even though he may not).

Financial Mail, 8 May 1998

Clear as fine-grained deposits, that is, mud

Jabulani Sikhakhane

Arthur Levitt, chairman of the Securities & Exchange Commission, holds strong opinions on obfuscation in corporate prospectuses.

'It is possible that no document on earth has committed as many sins against clear language as the prospectus. The prose trips off the tongue like peanut butter. Poetry seems to be reserved for claims about performance, and conciseness for discussions about fees,' he says.

The head of the US investor watchdog adds that much of this mysterious language is aimed at allaying legitimate legal concerns. But 'disclosure is not disclosure if it doesn't communicate'.

It is for this reason that the SEC will introduce a new rule on October 1 requiring that the cover page, summary and the section that discusses the company's risk factors in a prospectus – the document giving details of a forthcoming issue of shares – be written in plain English.

The SEC's plain English principles include definite, concrete, everyday words; tabular presentation of complex information and no legal jargon or technical business terms.

The US is no exception. The problem of companies submitting unintelligible documents to shareholders occurs all over the world.

In SA, a study by Plain Business Writing, a local consultancy run by former financial journalist Robert Gentle, has found that most investor documents – including circulars to shareholders, prospectuses, financial notices and annual reports – are characterized by 'formal language, complicated words, difficult-to-read print and poor layout'.

'The reader's first instinct is to file it, not read it,' says Gentle.

Through his consultancy, he is starting a campaign to clean up corporate SA's written communication. He has already been given the nod by regulatory authorities such as the Financial Services Board.

The ordinary, individual investor isn't the only one having trouble deciphering shareholder documents and other corporate announcements. Gentle tells a story of investment managers at a Cape-based assurer who spend each morning converting each company announcement into plain English.

But why do merchant bankers and corporate legal eagles write such convoluted documents to shareholders?

The answer is: they resort to 'legalese' as a cover in case legal action is taken against their clients. Common sense suggests, however, that ambiguity is a fertile breeding ground for litigation.

The other problem is that it seems most companies have forgotten the purpose of the disclosure requirements of corporate legislation and the various regulatory authorities such as the JSE and the Securities Regulation Panel.

These requirements are intended to keep the market informed. Compliance for its own sake is secondary to disclosure. But disclosure should also go beyond merely making information available. Such information should be easy to understand. Hence, the move towards plain English.

The campaign should be seen as part of the drive for better corporate governance in general, and the protection of shareholders' rights in particular.

What better way to safeguard those rights than to make sure that shareholders are kept well-informed of developments within – and sometimes outside – their company?

Most local companies seem to be ignoring the recommendations of the King committee on communicating with company stakeholders. In its corporate governance report published in 1994, the committee says communication must be open and easy to understand.

'The narrative of reporting is more important than what to the average investor is a complicated set of accounts and reports. It is of even greater importance in an SA of diverse cultures and emerging investors. The narrative must not only be open, but must be consistent and simple enough to be understandable to the average investor without sacrificing the quality of the information published,' says the committee, chaired by businessman Mervyn King.

The committee goes further. It raises an important aspect of communication: the need to strive for a balance between the positive and negative aspects of the company.

But most local prospectuses ignore this principle. This is particularly true of the small to medium-sized companies now flocking to the JSE, some without any solid track record. Such documents clearly spell out what the company's prospects are. But they don't explain in equal detail the risks to which the companies are exposed and the impact of such risks on the ability to meet the projected profits.

The prospectus of the Privest Group Ltd is a case in point. I single it out only because it is the most recent company to list. Its public offer of 10m shares attracted applications for more than 2,4bn shares.

In a full-page note, Privest's prospectus sets out the prospects for the group and why it believes it will deliver to its shareholders. It mentions that the profit forecast is based on assumptions that may not materialize. Such assumptions, including economic and political stability and changes in legislation, are not discussed in any detail.

But, shareholders, do not despair. There is a flicker of light at the end of the investment tunnel. The source of that light is the potential knock-on effect of SA's increasing integration into the world's financial markets.

As more and more local companies spread their tentacles overseas, they will have to meet far higher standards of disclosure.

Billiton Plc, the metals group that was spun off from Gencor last year, is a good example.

In its information memorandum to investors, including the local shareholders of Gencor, Billiton provided information about each of its business units that was remarkable on two counts – intelligibility and the amount of detail it provided, including the risks attached to each business unit.

Though for the moment the light flickers only faintly on the prospectuses of local companies, the investing public can look forward to enjoying its investment sandwich without sticky peanut butter one day.

Financial Mail, 10 December 1999

Deciphering the gobbledegook

James Eedes

If you think that shareholder documents should be read with a stiff drink to dull the pain, congratulate yourself you're reading them at all. Some investors dispatch these eyesores directly to the dustbin, says a readability survey.

Earlier this year, Rand Merchant Bank (RMB) and language consultants Plain Business Writing commissioned research company Markinor to give scientific credibility to something we've known all along – shareholder documents such as prospectuses, circulars and schemes of arrangement are a pain to wade through.

Interviews with lawyers, merchant bankers, investment analysts, stockbrokers, financial journalists and ordinary shareholders found – drum roll, please – that these documents are 'difficult to understand and way above the head of the average shareholder.' Anyone surprised?

The survey concludes that shareholder documents should be written in plain language using techniques such as summaries, standardised layouts and step-by-step explanations.

It's not such an outlandish idea – last year the US Securities and Exchange Commission (SEC) ruled that all new prospectuses there had to be published in plain English.

Still, respondents voiced concern that legality and the precise nature of documents might be compromised by more straightforward language. More than a quarter of respondents felt that 'dumbing down' would not make documents easier to understand.

One solution, the survey suggests, would be to provide a summary version in plain language, bundled in with the convoluted, legal-speak format. That way shareholders wouldn't be left in the dark and lawyers would have something that held up in court. Either way, RMB says the move towards simpler documents is just a matter of time.

An extract of the report mentioned in this article can be found on page 70.

The vital force in business life is the desire to serve.

George Eberhard
(quoted in Forbes Inc, 1997)

4

Write research reports

Then circulate them to your target market as a free service.

As we've already seen, the mere fact of your being a consultant makes you more knowledgeable about your field than almost anyone else. Put that knowledge to use by conducting research and writing up the findings in the form of a report.

If your research takes you to other countries, even better: nothing guarantees freshness and novelty like a first-hand account of how other countries are tackling a given issue. Write your report in plain language, with lots of summaries and descriptive headlines for easy scanning. Most important of all, make sure it has a one-page executive summary.

The finished document must be visually appealing, so have it designed, produced and printed by a professional design agency. It may cost a lot, but it's worth it. Unless you're an expert in layout and design, don't even think about doing it yourself. Also, remember to get your work edited by a good freelance editor or proofreader. Far too many expensively produced documents are full of spelling and grammatical errors.

HOW TO GET YOUR REPORTS NOTICED

Because you're in charge of the distribution of your report, the scope for really innovative publicity techniques is huge. After all, who knows your market better than you? Here's a basic three-step programme that will get you results:

- Step 1
  Determine your target audience: build a database of every person you think should be reading this report.
- Step 2
  Post or hand-deliver the report to your target audience. It should be accompanied by a short covering letter of no more than three paragraphs. Do *not* tout for business in the letter; you could, however, say that you'd be happy to come and give a presentation on the subject.
- Step 3
  Arrange media coverage. Write a press release of no more than two pages summarizing the report. Then send the release, along with the report, to those business publications you know are likely to run the story. Send it to the business desks of your local radio and TV stations too.

DON'T CHARGE FOR YOUR REPORTS

Tempting though it undoubtedly is, resist the temptation to charge people for your report. Remember, this kind of publication is a long-term investment in your public profile, not a short-term moneymaking venture. Your immediate objective should be to have as many copies of the report as possible floating around the market.

Grasp the subject; the words will follow.

Cato the Elder, 234–149 BC
(quoted in Ratcliffe, 2000)

HERE'S A REPORT WITH A DIFFERENCE

A report isn't the only thing of value you can send your target market. Have you ever thought of publishing your own small pocket directory (20 to 50 pages) of key players in your market sector? You could send it free of charge to existing and potential clients. It beats sending diaries or pens any day. Any reputable design agency could easily handle such a job. Your directory, prominently branded with your company name and logo, would feature categories such as research institutes, relevant magazines and newspapers, relevant government departments, the relevant regulatory authorities, major players and even – yes! – other consultancies.

EXAMPLES OF RESEARCH REPORTS

When I started my plain language consultancy, my biggest problem was a lack of knowledge of the subject in the South African financial services industry, my main target market. I clearly had to educate the industry on various aspects of the subject before I could hope to sell them my services. Here are three reports I wrote that neatly solved the problem:

- **Plain language in financial services**
  South Africa trails the rest of the world (22 pages)
  To get the information for this report, I surfed the Internet, fixed interviews and then flew to London for a four-day visit. There, I met representatives from UK banks, legal firms, insurance companies, the Inland Revenue and the regulatory authorities. The subsequent report was featured in virtually every mainstream business publication and was frequently requested by businesspeople who had read about it. About 800 copies of the 1,000-copy print run were distributed.

- **Plain language prospectuses**
  What we can learn from the US (22 pages)
  This report also required an overseas trip, this time to Washington, DC, to visit the Securities and Exchange Commission (SEC), which was spearheading a drive towards clear, user-friendly prospectuses. One interview and a couple of hours in their library were all I needed, and I flew back with loads of useful information. The report was sent to all the leading investment banks and stockbroking firms on my target list, and was featured prominently in the media. As a result, one of the country's leading investment banks adopted a plain language programme – and retained me as the consultant.
- **Findings of a study into the readability of shareholder documents (16 pages)**
  The idea was to conduct a research study involving a sample of 24 lawyers, stockbrokers, analysts, shareholders and financial journalists. However, it was too expensive for me to do alone, so I persuaded a leading investment bank to put up part of the cost in exchange for being associated with it. The finished document was sent to hundreds of influential people, received extensive media coverage, was mentioned at international conferences and was reviewed in a US legal journal. It was also requested, via the bank's Web site, from as far afield as Hong Kong and Australia (see page 70 for an extract from the report).

The all-in cost of researching, designing and printing each report was more than compensated for by the heightened public profile and new business it produced. Best of all, the publication of these reports shifted the balance of effort: instead of me contacting companies for consulting work, they started to contact me. At the end of the day, that's what it's all about – getting them to come to you.

If you are reading the sports page, where do you want to see the result of yesterday's cup final – up front in the headline or way down in the last paragraph? Reports are no different: your reader wants the conclusion right away, not on page 11 after thousands of words describing why the report was written and the intricacies of the methodology.

Robert Gentle
(2001: 125)

EXTRACT FROM REPORT

The following pages contain the executive summary and first two chapters of a report entitled 'Findings of a study into the readability of shareholder documents'.

Note how the report has deliberately been written for busy people who need to catch key points at a glance. This explains:

- the report's central finding right up front on the cover;
- lots of descriptive headlines to facilitate scanning;
- an upfront summary of every chapter *before* the detail.

Findings of a study into the readability of shareholder documents

Most respondents agreed
that they are complicated and
should be written in plain language

RAND MERCHANT BANK

Tel (27 11) 282-8404
Fax (27 11) 282-1047
E-mail *maureen.gleeson@rmb.co.za*
Website *www.rmb.co.za*

Plain Business Writing

Tel (27 11) 881-5570
Fax (27 11) 881-5540
E-mail *query@plainwriting.co.za*
Website *www.plainwriting.co.za*

Contact us for more information or if you would like additional copies

Study done by Markinor

This report is based on the findings of a study done
in May 1999 by Markinor, a South African research firm.

The study was commissioned by Rand Merchant Bank,
a South African investment bank, and Plain Business
Writing, a South African plain language consultancy.

Cross-section of people interviewed

Markinor conducted separate interviews with 24 lawyers,
merchant bankers, investment analysts, stockbrokers,
financial journalists and ordinary shareholders.

They were shown various shareholder documents, both
traditional and simplified, and asked for their comments.

Contents

Scintillate, scintillate,
globule vivific
How I do ponder
thy nature specific

(Twinkle, twinkle,
little star
How I wonder
what you are . . .)

Executive summary

Most respondents agreed that shareholder documents are complicated, and that they should be written in plain language as long as legal accuracy is not compromised

Shareholder documents are complicated

Shareholder documents such as prospectuses, circulars and schemes of arrangement are considered difficult to understand. They are way above the head of the average shareholder. One doubts whether they are understood or even read by the layperson. Some investors just throw them straight into the dustbin.

They should be written in plain language

Shareholder documents should be written in plain language using techniques such as:

- plain words
- short sentences
- descriptive headlines
- a summary or synopsis
- step-by-step explanations
- a standardised layout.

Maintain legal accuracy, don't leave anything out

While it is important for shareholder documents to be readable, care should be taken not to omit pertinent information or compromise legal accuracy. Summaries or abridged versions of the document should not be separated from the main document; readers should not get the impression that they do not need to read the rest of the document.

What respondents thought of traditional shareholder documents

Most found these documents difficult to understand
and doubt whether shareholders even read them

What the study says

"Generally, respondents agreed that shareholder documents are
complicated and time-consuming to read . . . There is little doubt
that most shareholder documents are perceived to be way above
the head of the individual shareholder. In fact, many respondents
said they doubt whether they are understood or even read by the
average layperson."

Majority view

**Ordinary investors find shareholder documents longwinded,
overly technical and difficult to understand.**

1. *"These documents are not user-friendly to the man in the street."*
    (JSE/SRP)

2. *"Generally very difficult. [They] seem to have been put together
    just to fulfil the legal imperative."* (investment analyst)

3. *"[The] vast majority of shareholders don't even bother with
    them. They are just too complicated."* (shareholder)

4. *"[It is] quite difficult for unsophisticated investors to understand
    what is going on. Some just throw the whole thing in the
    dustbin."* (lawyer)

5. *"To read this and understand what is going on requires time.
    Part of the problem is that most people just don't have time."*
    (lawyer)

Minority view

**Shareholder documents may be difficult to understand, but they
must meet regulatory and legal requirements.**

1. *"I would like to think that the regulators are trying to pass on all
    information and at the same time [make the document]
    readable."* (JSE/SRP)

2. *"There are stock exchange requirements. [I] don't think you
    could do it much shorter."* (lawyer)

What respondents thought of plain language shareholder documents

They overwhelmingly supported such documents
in the interests of readability

What the study says

"With only one or two exceptions, the people interviewed seemed
convinced that a move towards plain language documents would
be a very positive development."

Majority view

**Plain language is a must if we want investors to read and
understand shareholder documents.**

1. *"I believe that for a shareholder to make some selection, it is
   incredibly important for [a document] to be in plain language."*
   (JSE/SRP)

2. *"If companies want to move towards a broader shareholder
   base, this is definitely the way to go."* (JSE/SRP)

3. *"It has to happen. It would make life easier."* (stockbroker)

4. *"Active voice and descriptive headings I agree with. We should
   all strive to make our documents more simple."* (lawyer)

5. *"This is the future, the way to go. Shareholders will know
   exactly what is going on and will not need to bug us."*
   (stockbroker)

6. *"If [the document] is in plain language, [shareholders] will
   probably read through even a thick prospectus."* (JSE/SRP)

Minority view

**Plain language is desirable, but it may get in the way of legal
accuracy.**

1. *"[I'm] not sure how you are going to get around all the legalities
   by using ordinary language."* (stockbroker)

2. *"Clarity is needed. To try and draft statutes, contracts and
   regulations in a chatty sort of way is dangerous."* (lawyer)

In America, only the successful writer is important, in France all writers are important, in England no writer is important, in Australia you have to explain what a writer is.

Geoffrey Cotterell
(quoted in Metcalf, 1986: 272)

5

Write a book

Try to get into print: few things bestow authority and credibility like authorship.

You can, as a consultant, write a fairly interesting book on your area of expertise. It may not qualify for the Pulitzer Prize, and your grandchildren probably won't want you to read it aloud to them, but your clients will be grateful you wrote it.

What makes you qualified to write? Expertise and experience. Been there, done that is your calling card. You've been in the trenches, fought the battles, made the mistakes. What will you write about? Whatever it is that you find you're particularly good at or original at. You'll know deep inside just what that is, and you'll know it with a level of certainty that may astound you. It doesn't matter if there already are books out there on the subject; just make sure yours takes a fresh, new perspective.

Your book doesn't have to be long, complex or erudite. In fact, the shorter and simpler, the better. Make it practical and user-friendly so that people find it genuinely useful. You want this to be a how-to book, not a textbook.

The decision to write this particular book came to me over coffee with a fellow consultant who had just asked me how she should go about generating new business. Not surprisingly, her cold-calling was not yielding any results. I rattled off what to me were the obvious things to do, and she scribbled away furiously, grateful for the advice. Then it suddenly hit me: this wasn't the first time I'd been asked by consultants for advice on marketing themselves – I really should do a book on it! That very afternoon, flushed with excitement, I put all other work on hold and did an outline of the book. I then went to a couple of bookshops to see if anything similar had been done before. Nothing – the field seemed to be wide open. A few days later, I wrote the first chapter, and decided to devote two mornings a week to the project. A month later, it was done.

HOW TO GET PUBLISHED

Whom to approach? Simply go to the business section of your nearest bookshop, locate books similar to the one you're planning to write and note down the details of the publisher. How to prepare your proposal and manuscript? For pointers, read one of the many good how-to-get-yourself-published books out there. Here are some well-known titles that you can find in any major bookstore in the English-speaking world:

- *Writers' and Artists' Yearbook*, published annually (A & C Black) and *The Writer's Handbook,* edited by Barry Turner and published annually (Macmillan). Both these well-known books contain informative lists of publishing houses, agents and the kind of manuscripts they handle.
- *From Pitch to Publication: Everything you need to know to get your novel published*, Carol Blake (Macmillan). Although pitched at writers of novels, this excellent book, written by an agent, contains a wealth of information on how the publishing industry works. The chapter on contracts is particularly useful.

Alternatively, if you've already located a potential publisher to approach, visit that publisher's Web site and check the submission requirements for first-time authors. Then sit down and write the book – the whole book; first-time authors don't get very far with only a three-chapter outline.

I asked my publisher what would happen if he sold all the copies of my book he had printed. He said, 'I'll just print another ten.'

Eric Sykes
(quoted in MacHale, 1997: 56)

GETTING PUBLISHED REQUIRES LOTS OF PATIENCE

Writing your book will be the easy part. Getting someone to publish it is where the difficulty starts. The hard truth is that it's a publisher's market out there, and the odds are heavily stacked in their favour from a supply-and-demand perspective. There are simply more manuscripts floating around the world market than there are publishers willing or able to publish them, so a ruthless weeding-out process takes place. Manuscripts pile up on desks and it takes a long time – about six to eight weeks – for publishers to get back to you; some may not even bother. As for agents, it's just not worth the effort: they hardly ever take on first-time writers of non-fiction. However, persevere. After all, those experts whose books you see in bookshops started off as first-time authors too, and they successfully cracked the system. If they can do it, so can you.

Checklist

How to maximize your chances of getting published

- Choose a subject no one else has written about – or at least bring a fresh, original angle to it.

- Write in plain, conversational language; avoid heavy academic writing.

- Estimate, as reliably as possible, the market for your book; publishers are in the business of making money and like books with big sales potential.

- Research the publishing industry to see who publishes what before deciding which firm to send your proposal to; even the best manuscript is worthless in the hands of the wrong publisher.

- Your proposal must be short (two to four pages), punchy and persuasive; it's the first indication the publisher has of your ability to put a point across.

CONSIDER PUBLISHING YOUR OWN WORK

If you can't get a traditional publisher to publish your book, but still have an unshakeable confidence in its sales potential, then consider publishing and distributing it yourself. This runs contrary to the advice offered to would-be authors by virtually every how-to-get-published book, but these books have not always given much thought to the peculiarities of consulting. After all, consultants have a defined target market that they can easily reach without the help of a retail bookshop. Moreover, they can achieve economies of scale on a print run of barely 2,000 copies, a figure that traditional publishing houses aren't always able to match.

For example, if you're a healthcare consultant and you want to write a short guide on how companies can implement an in-house corporate fitness programme linked to employees' pay, then you know exactly whom to sell it to – the HR director of every company in the land. You probably deal with many of these people anyway.

Acting as your own publisher is as simple as handing your manu-script to any reputable design agency (probably the one you use for your promotional material) and asking them to print it as a kind of longer-than-usual report in soft-cover format. Also, remember the following:

- Apply for an ISBN (International Standard Book Number) from the national library in your area; once they've faxed or e-mailed it to you, ask the design agency to have it bar-coded on the back cover.

*Give a man a fish and you feed him for a day;
teach a man to fish and you have a 12-part series,
a book and two or three videos.*

(BBC, 1998)

- Include the standard copyright and ownership warnings before the contents page (take your cue from the standard clauses in existing business books).
- Use a professional book editor (many work on a freelance basis) to proof your book and turn it into a good, easy read.
- Ask your most favoured, reputable clients to provide you with short reviews (20 words maximum), which you can then put on the back cover.
- Write a catchy, persuasive blurb for the back cover – and also include a short biography summarizing your consulting experience.
- Choose a realistic print run, ie one that's big enough to cover your target market, but not so big that you end up sitting with thousands of copies of unsold stock.

Once you've got your books, you can sell them directly to your existing clients. You can even try for the best of both worlds and approach bookshops to see if they'd like to stock your title. Although you'd make most of your sales yourself, the bookshops would add a welcome degree of visibility. Limit yourself to a handful of high-profile bookshops to avoid the time-consuming administrative hassle of keeping them adequately stocked with your titles.

How do you decide whether you should consider publishing your own book? If the subject matter has the following characteristics, then give it some serious thought:

- It addresses a real need.
- It's too long to be a report, but too short to be a traditional book (eg 50 to 100 pages).
- It has a readily identifiable corporate readership (eg secretaries, managers, finance directors).

My enthusiasm for self-publishing flows from a series of short business writing books that I published (see brochure on page 166). About 50 to 75 pages long and costing £5 to £10 each, they

Hitler's original title for Mein Kampf *was* Four and a Half Years of Struggle against Lies, Stupidity and Cowardice. *Everyone needs an editor.*

Tim Foote
(quoted in MacHale, 1996: 150)

covered specific areas of business writing such as letters, reports, legal contracts and annual reports. Over 12,000 copies were sold to about 900 companies. More to the point, a lot of consulting business and lecture opportunities were generated as a result of the exposure.

HOW TO GET YOUR BOOK NOTICED

If your book is published through the usual channels, most of your initial publicity will be orchestrated by your publisher through a launch event, maybe a book signing at stores and almost certainly some media coverage. However, that doesn't stop you from promoting the book yourself after the launch by organizing your own talks, presentations and media coverage, or sending copies to potential clients. If you published the book yourself, of course you should be doing all of this anyway.

You'll find that the book will considerably enhance your status and make it easier for you to win new business. John Brown, consultant and author, has a very authoritative ring to it! This is particularly true on the conference circuit, where authors are particularly welcome because it is assumed – rightly, in most cases – that they must know something the rest of us don't. Pick up any corporate conference programme, take a look at the qualifications of the speakers and you'll see that at least a handful of them have written books.

WHAT KIND OF BOOKS TO WRITE

The trick is to focus on problems and solutions, rather than to wax lyrical about your subject in an open-ended manner. So go for books such as 'Five ways to...' or 'Seven things wrong with...' or 'How to... in three easy steps'. A cursory glance at the shelves of major bookshops shows that this approach is quite common.

Being published by the Oxford University Press is rather like being married to a duchess: the honour is greater than the pleasure.

G M Young
(quoted in MacHale, 1996: 146)

KEEP YOUR TITLES TITILLATING!

A word about titles: make sure they are catchy and intriguing. Boring titles are the kiss of death. More than one observer has noted that *The Ancient Mariner* would not have sold as many copies if it had been called *The Old Sailor*. And as a newspaper columnist wryly observed: 'The two most important words in *Last Tango in Paris* are tango and Paris, both of which are regarded as sophisticated and adult. *Last Hokey-Cokey in Macclesfield* wouldn't be the same at all' (Mark Steyn in Jarski, 2000).

Examples
Table 5.1 gives examples of subjects for books.

Table 5.1 *What you could write a book on*

You're a consultant in	You could write a book on
information technology	Improve your Web site *The 10 things people hate most about Web sites – and how to fix them*
employee well-being	Pay them to be healthy *How to implement a complete staff fitness programme using financial incentives*
architecture	Open those windows *And other easy ways to a healthier work environment*
costs	Keep costs down *How to reduce the cost of phone calls, photocopying and other in-house services*
training	Read 'em and reap *Reward your staff financially for reading books and subscribing to important magazines*
security	Stop, thief! *50 ways companies expose themselves to theft – and how to fix it within a week*

I do not object to people looking at their watches when I am speaking – but I strongly object when they start shaking them to make certain they are still going.

Lord Birkett
(quoted in Metcalf, 1986: 240)

6

Hit the lecture circuit

If you've got something interesting to say, people will want to hear it.

Ex-presidents do it, so why not you? The lecture circuit need not be the exclusive preserve of politicians past their prime; it is the ideal platform for you as a consultant to hold forth on your particular area of expertise.

Don't expect to be paid vast amounts of money, though – at least not until you've achieved a degree of fame and celebrity. In any event, your real aim in hitting the lecture circuit is not to earn speaker fees, but to invest in your public profile and bring your knowledge to the attention of potential clients. The key word here is knowledge – don't make a sales pitch; give an interesting, informative and objective presentation.

For example, a healthcare consultant might talk about the health risks of air-conditioned buildings and their effect on productivity; an educational consultant might talk about why exposing toddlers to the Internet may stunt their ability to socialize in the real world. In short, it's the kind of thing you might read about in a magazine or see in a TV report and say 'Hey, that's interesting; I had no idea!'

The beauty about public speaking is that it is not a one-off thing. If you've got a presentation that's genuinely interesting, you can use it time and time again, either in its original form or slightly adapted to the needs of your audience. As long as it remains topical and meaningful, and audiences love it, it can run for many seasons – much like a good Broadway play.

WHERE TO SPEAK

There are a number of public platforms that work very well for consultants. Of course, some are more easily accessible than others. Here are the three you should be focusing on:

- **Companies.** Go and visit the companies you'd like to have as clients and give your presentation directly to executives, directors, managers, secretaries or whichever particular audience you're interested in reaching. Typically, you'd give these talks in the company boardroom or auditorium, depending on the size of your audience.
- **Corporate getaways.** Once a year, key categories of staff (eg senior management, marketing, IT) go on getaways to some exotic location where they review their strategic direction – and then play lots of golf. It's not unusual for consultants to be invited to give a talk on some or other aspect of the proceedings.
- **Conferences.** The corporate calendar in every major city in the world is chock-a-block with conferences where, as a consultant, you can muscle in as a speaker. You are spoilt for choice, as these conferences cover virtually every industry sector (mining, banking, advertising, etc) and every key area of corporate activity (marketing, telesales, emotional intelligence, etc).

The importance of a public speaker bears an inverse relationship to the number of microphones into which he speaks.

William Morgan
(quoted in MacHale, 1997: 120)

FIRST DEVISE A SLICK PRESENTATION

Every good public talk revolves around a presentation, so fire up your laptop and build a really good presentation around your particular area of expertise. Your basic talk should be 30 minutes long, but you need to be able to shorten or lengthen it to suit the occasion. For example, while a conference might ask you to expand your presentation to 45 minutes, a board of directors would almost certainly ask you to cut it to 15 minutes or less. Flexibility is the key.

Remember that slick does not mean over the top. Make sure your presentation is well structured and easy to follow. And watch the verbiage. Don't do a mind-dump on each of your slides; rather limit yourself to a few key points that your audience can take in at a glance.

Finally, you the person, rather than the technological wizardry of your slides, are the ultimate measure of how successful your presentation is. As the saying goes, a fool with a tool is still a fool. That means mastering the basics of public speaking: know your subject, relate to your audience, speak confidently, and use wit and humour if you can. If you are a terrible – or terrified – speaker, go on a presentation skills course. Better still, join Toastmasters, because you'll get the opportunity to practise. Whatever you do, don't inflict yourself on an audience if you can't hold their attention; it could be the kiss of death for your business.

Checklist

Structure your talk to suit your audience

- less than15 minutes: time-pressured directors;
- 15 to 30 minutes: managers, executives, staff;
- 30 to 60 minutes: conference delegates;
- one to three hours: workshop delegates.

HOW TO GET INVITED TO SPEAK

Ask. It's that simple. There's a conference coming up on branding, and you're a branding specialist? Contact the organizers and suggest that your talk be considered. You run into the head of IT of a big corporation at a cocktail function and you hear her outline a particular problem that just happens to be right up your street? Tell her you'd be happy to come over and give her staff a short presentation on the subject.

Alternatively, you could be a lot more methodical: draw up a list of companies and conferences you'd like to speak at, and send them an e-mail, letter or brochure explaining your talk and availability. Don't worry about rejections: sooner or later someone will take you up on your offer – it's a numbers game. And remember that organizers of conferences and other corporate getaways are always looking for speakers. Far from nagging them or being intrusive, you're actually doing them a big favour by proactively contacting them.

Here's an example of a talk that I successfully pitched to the International Association of Business Communicators (IABC) so that I could be a speaker at their annual conference in 2001 in New York (see page 108 for an excerpt from this presentation):

Subject of talk
The human factor in business communication
Just because you've written something – a report, brochure, proposal or whatever – doesn't mean your intended reader will actually read it. Why? Human nature – the tendency to take the path of least resistance.

Several factors conspire against you – the time your reader has, whether you know him personally, his level of interest, how urgent the document is, whether it can be scanned, the presence of alternative versions of the message and the general lack of any negative consequences for just ignoring it altogether.

This talk looks at how these critical factors influence key categories of business communication (correspondence, reports/

Cardinal Sin 10: never accept a booking in Pennyslvania.

...Or Wisconsin or Minnesota or the Dakotas. As a tribe, they... are bereft of a sense of humor... Pray for an audience of urban Jews, Irish, Spaniards, Poles, and Trappist Monks. (They laugh at anything.)

Reid Buckley
(1999)

proposals and promotional literature) and what you can do to limit their effects.

Later, as your public profile increases and your market reputation becomes established, you may find yourself being invited to give a talk. This is especially true if you happen to be an entertaining speaker, because you then add an extra dimension to the rather clinical one of mere knowledge and expertise.

Opinion pieces that you may write for the business press are particularly successful in generating speaking invitations because, by definition, they contain the outline of a possible conference topic. It's no secret that conference organizers regularly trawl through newspapers and magazines looking for interesting articles, opinion pieces and letters to the editor.

I was once invited to address an international executive secretaries conference on the subject of plain language simply because the conference organizer had seen an article of mine on the subject in a business magazine. The organizer paid for my flight as well as my accommodation at a luxury hotel, and I had a pleasant day away from the office and the opportunity to meet new clients – not a bad return on investment for one simple article that took a couple of hours to write.

Sometimes, you don't even have to be particularly well known to catch the attention of a conference organizer; all you have to do is say the right thing at the right time. Some fairly innocuous business observations I once e-mailed to a US consultant made such an impact that she invited me to speak on the subject the following year at a conference in Houston, Texas.

Checklist

Where to find news of upcoming conferences

- industry and umbrella bodies;
- professional conference organizations;
- convention and exhibition centres;

Yes, about ten minutes.

Duke of Wellington
[responding to a vicar's enquiry as to whether
there was anything he would like the forthcoming
sermon to be about]
(quoted in The Times, *2000)*

- leading hotels;

- specialist trade magazines;

- the mainstream press.

COMPANIES VERSUS CONFERENCES

In-company presentations beat conference presentations any day. Conferences are certainly worth chasing and are excellent in producing new business leads, but you don't always reach the right level of client representative, or indeed a sufficiently large number of them.

It's far simpler and more effective to go directly to your target company and do your presentation there. After all, that's where the business is. You end up face to face with the people who have the responsibility and the budget for employing your services. Over a two-year period, I did about 50 in-company presentations compared to only about five conferences. The conferences may have been more glamorous and exciting, but it was the company presentations that brought in the business – sometimes the very next day.

If you want to get into companies, don't forget to network, network, network! Relationships greatly increase the likelihood that you'll be invited to speak. So join associations and industry bodies. More to the point, attend their cocktails, talks and other networking functions, even though you'd probably prefer to give them a miss, go home and watch a sitcom on TV instead.

| **Checklist** |

How to get into a company

Consider contacting the following support services departments because they are heavy users of outside skills and like to share what they've learnt with management:

- human resources;
- training;
- marketing;
- public relations;
- information technology.

RUN YOUR OWN WORKSHOPS

To get more mileage out of your short 30-minute presentation, try fleshing it out into a two- to three-hour workshop, complete with exercises and case studies. You could then run your own workshop sessions and charge for them.

Alternatively, you could approach an industry association or umbrella body and get them to organize the event for their members. They do all the legwork, send out the invitations and organize the venue. You, the invited guest, just show up and do your thing. Why should associations help you out in this way? Enlightened self-interest: industry associations are duty-bound to run training events for their members, but don't always know whom to approach – or don't have the budget to attract real talent. So resist the temptation to ask too much money for such events; take the bare minimum that covers your costs. Remember: the big prize for you is a captive audience of representatives from your target market. Even if you did it for nothing, it would still probably be worth it. You can't put a price on exposure.

DO ROADSHOWS OUT OF TOWN

Whether you work in New York, London or Johannesburg, you will almost certainly not want to limit your business activities to those

It wasn't my finest hour. It wasn't even my finest half-hour.

Bill Clinton
[remembering an overlong speech]
(quoted in The Times, 2000)

particular cities. Consultancy travels easily, and there's no reason why you shouldn't also be working in Boston, Birmingham or Cape Town. Roadshow presentations are a great way of introducing yourself to new business prospects in other cities. Inform a number of companies that you'll be in town on such and such a date to give a presentation, and you'll be surprised at how many of them agree to see you. The reason is distance, and the traditional hospitality we tend to extend to out-of-towners: people are less likely to refuse to see someone who's just flown in from somewhere else. Peer pressure helps too. Let's say there are five companies in another city you'd like to sign on. The trick is to contact the relevant person at Company 1, say you'll be down there for a day to present to Company 2, Company 3, Company 4 and Company 5, and would it be OK if you popped in as well? You should bag at least three out of the five. Works every time.

EXAMPLE OF A CONFERENCE PRESENTATION

About the conference

It was the 2001 annual convention of the IABC (International Association of Business Communicators). The conference was held at the New York Hilton over four days and featured about 1,500 delegates and over 80 speakers. The large number of speakers reflects the fact that it was a seven-track conference, ie there were seven talks running at any one time. Speakers had an unusually long one-and-a-quarter-hour slot for their presentation, even though most finished well before that. (The conference has a reputation for covering issues in some depth.)

About the presentation

This is the talk referred to earlier in this chapter on page 99. Here's how it was presented in the conference programme:

Effective written communication: overcoming the human factor. Just because you've written something doesn't mean it will be read. Why not? Human nature – people tend to take the path of least resistance. In this session, you'll learn:

- to identify the human factors that make ignoring your document an attractive proposition;
- how each of these factors affects an individual's 'decision to read';
- how to write a document that works with, not against, human nature.

Notice the following:

- The attention-grabbing opening slide about the movie theatre experiment – even before the agenda is unveiled.
- Some of the slides are clearly intriguing while others are boringly clinical; but what they have in common is simplicity and brevity.
- The easy, conversational speaking style, with a clear emphasis on short, staccato-type sentences.
- The speaker doesn't merely repeat what's on each slide, but develops the slide's central message with relevant observations.
- The humour is contextual, not gratuitous; in other words, it has been woven naturally into the subject matter, and therefore doesn't come across as contrived.

Analyse this!

The human factor in business communication

ROBERT GENTLE

Thank you.

Good morning, everyone.

Let's get started by going to the movies.

Cry me a river...

Many years ago, researchers performed an interesting experiment into the nature of crying. They put about 20 people side by side in a single row of a private cinema, gave them a seriously large box of tissues and showed them a real tear-jerker.

But guess what? Virtually nobody cried.

Turns out it was because the subjects had been sitting side by side, too close together. [MOVE ELBOWS APPROPRIATELY] Not enough privacy.

The experiment was repeated, but this time the subjects were allowed to sit anywhere. Without exception, they spread themselves around, a good few rows and seat spaces apart.

This time they bawled their hearts out.

Human nature. Never overlook it. Not even in your business writing. That's the subject of our talk today.

CONTENTS

- **Human nature**

- **The 'decision to read'**

- **Examples of good documents**

That's our agenda:

What is human nature?

How does it affect the decision to read?

How do we get around it in our documents?

Human nature

Capricious OR predictable?

The Oxford Dictionary defines 'capricious' as 'inconstant, readily swayed by whim or fancy'.

Is human nature capricious?

Or is it governed by certain rules?

Well, let's see.

Trains, planes and automobiles

Show me where I'm going –
not where I've been

Next time you're in a train with forward-facing and backward-facing seats, notice how most people sit.

They prefer to face forward, in the direction of travel. Not backwards – even though this is by far the safer option in case of a crash.

Same thing in planes.

Airlines once experimented with backward-facing seats for safety reasons, but this never really caught on. Passengers want to see where they're going, not where they've come from.

Human nature.

[ASIDE] Those of you who travel regularly to London may have noticed that British Airways have started to offer backward-facing sleeper seats in first and business class. It'll be interesting to see if this works or flops.

Let's go shopping.

You want my money?

Let me touch and feel!

Walk into a computer store and you'll see that all the CD ROMs are wrapped in plastic and packed in boxes.

But go to Saks or Bloomingdales, and you'll see that all the fabrics – linen, clothes, towels – are left unwrapped. Even the really expensive lines.

Why do you think that is? [PROMPT AUDIENCE]

So that people can touch them. We're tactile. We need to physically experience anything that comes into contact with our skin – otherwise we rip off the packaging.

Human nature.

These two examples show that we aren't just a bunch of robots who do whatever we're told.

We often react in unexpected ways – and there's nothing haphazard or capricious about it.

Human nature is predictable, and underpinned by desire for

- excitement
- sense of discovery
- security
- comfort
- emotional well-being

These are the more obvious factors we can all relate to – even those of us who have never been in therapy.

[DEPENDING ON REACTION] *And for those of you who are contemplating therapy, please remember the difference between a psychologist and a psychiatrist. A psychiatrist has the authority to lock you away for the rest of your life, but a psychologist can only ask you how you feel.*

There's a critical human-nature factor not on this list. It is central to how we process written information.

A stockbroker would call it: buying low and selling high. A marketer would call it getting maximum bang for your buck.

The engineer in me likes to call it operational efficiency – minimum input, maximum output.

Human nature also about operational efficiency

maximum output

minimum input

Human beings are hard-wired to reduce the energy needed for any given task.

That's why I'm standing up here with a clip-on mic rather than a heavy hand-held number – and you're listening to me seated comfortably in chairs, not standing on your heads doing yoga.

Mind you, there's a fine line between saving energy and not wanting to expend it in the first place. As Joan Rivers once remarked: I hate housework. You make the beds; you do the dishes; then six months later you have to start all over again.

Operational efficiency is a normal biological function. What does it mean in practice?

Operational efficiency in practice

- Too hot? We look for **shade**
- Too **busy**? We multi-task
- Too far? We cut **corners**

It's about saving time and effort.

Show me a garden path with a 90-degree turn and I'll show you footmarks on the lawn. Nobody turns a corner at right angles (DEMONSTRATE BY WALKING AWKWARDLY). It's biologically inefficient.

Welcome to the path of least resistance.

Business writing and the path of least resistance

- We want the message with **minimal effort**
- We have a '**frustration**' threshold
- We can choose to **ignore** it

[MIMIC HEADBUTTING ON DESK] That's how most of us feel when confronted with yet another turgid business document.

Reading is a voluntary exercise.

You can lead a horse to water, but you can't force it to drink. You can put a business document under someone's nose, but you can't force them to read it.

The person has to want to read it.

Hence the term 'decision to read', which is best defined in the form of a question:

The decision to read

or

*'Why the **hell** should I
even be bothering with this?'*

Business documents are a necessary evil, not a literary feast we
eagerly delight in.

*Nobody picks up a memo and says: 'Wow, will you look at that
sentence in the second paragraph – that is so Hemingway!'*

*Nobody goes out in the middle of the night to look for IBM's annual
report because they want something to read. [PAUSE] Well, perhaps
some people do, but they're usually recaptured very quickly... and
taken back to the sanitorium.*

What are the factors that influence our decision to read? Time is
obviously one of them. There are at least nine others.

[PROMPT AUDIENCE]

Key factors that influence the 'decision to read'

- Do I have the **time**?
- Do I know **who** sent this?
- Is this **interesting**?
- Is this **relevant**?
- Is this **important**?   .../

[DISCUSS]

These are some of the questions that run through our mind.

To fully utilize the strengths of trade shows, [one] must do more than just show up.

J Thomas Russell and W Ronald Lane
(1998)

7

Promote yourself at trade exhibitions

This is useful if you have a product or service that actually needs to be seen.

WHAT IS A TRADE EXHIBITION?

As the name implies, it's an event where companies in a particular area of trade exhibit their wares. Trade exhibitions take place in huge indoor halls the size of aircraft hangars, and feature hundreds of stands where companies show off their products and services. Virtually every industry sector has its annual trade show, and the corporate calendar is chock-a-block with them. Some well-known examples are:

- Frankfurt Book Fair (Germany) – publishing;
- ASTD Expo (USA) – corporate training;
- Comdex (USA) – IT/computers;
- Earls Court Motor Show (UK) – automobiles.

Tens of thousands of visitors troop through these exhibitions. Brochures fly off the stands, business cards are passed out and business deals are lined up or concluded. It's a tiring, exhausting affair for both visitor and exhibitor alike, but it can be a good investment in time and effort.

WHERE TO FIND OUT ABOUT THEM

Just call up your local exhibition centre and ask for the programme of events for the year; it's that simple. These days, every half-decent town or city has at least one major exhibition centre. Olympia in London is one such centre; the Parc des Expositions in Paris is another. More often than not, exhibition halls are part of a convention centre. This allows for an exhibition and a conference in any given field to run at the same time, often as part of the same overall industry event. Many of the larger hotels (eg Intercontinental, Hilton, Sheraton) also host exhibitions as add-ons to the numerous conferences held there.

WHAT KIND OF CONSULTANT USES EXHIBITIONS?

There are two key categories of consultants who should consider financing a stand at a trade exhibition: 1) those with a specific product that can be bought and taken away (eg a line of books or CD ROMs); and 2) those with a computer-based application that needs to be viewed to be understood (eg a financial planning package or a database application).

If you fall into either of these categories, then an exhibition would give you the opportunity to showcase your product or service to potential clients, and to give them your latest promotional literature. It might well result in immediate sales, or at the very least a few strong leads that could be converted later into a big contract.

If, on the other hand, all you sell is your time, you'd be hard-pressed to justify setting up a stand. After all, what would you exhibit?

*There is no such thing as soft sell and hard sell.
There is only smart sell and stupid sell.*

*Charles Browder
Former president of BBDO
(quoted in Woods, 2000)*

THE PROS AND CONS OF TRADE EXHIBITIONS

The pros are:

- networking;
- meeting potential clients;
- generating sales leads;
- shifting your promotional literature;
- selling yourself in person.

The cons are:

- high cost (a 3m × 3m stand could set you back £1,000 to £2,000, and that doesn't include the design of the stand itself, and the temporary staff you'll have to hire to help you manage it);
- time away from the office (you're effectively out of circulation for the duration of the exhibition);
- poor attendance (the conference may pull in fewer people than expected, or the wrong calibre of people);
- information overload (everyone who visits your stand has already visited at least a hundred others, and may not be totally receptive to your message);
- sheer exhaustion (staying on your feet all day and being nice to all those people can be physically and emotionally draining);
- follow-up work (when you get back to the office, you've got to respond to all those requests for information that you got during the exhibition).

ORGANIZERS USUALLY HELP FIRST-TIME EXHIBITORS

Don't worry if you're clueless about how to make the most of an exhibition: a good organizer will always host a comprehensive

Every sale has five basic obstacles: no need, no money, no hurry, no desire, no trust.

Zig Ziglar
(quoted in Woods, 2000)

briefing session for all exhibitors. This is like an idiot's guide to making your stand a success, and is invariably run by an exhibition 'veteran' with years of experience. He or she will show a detailed slide presentation, followed by a video or two containing tips, useful advice and common mistakes to avoid.

Checklist

Tips from the front line

- Design your stand so that it can be taken in at a glance, like a billboard on a highway.

- Always have enough temporary help to handle huge inflows of people through your stand.

- Train your temporary assistants to answer customer queries intelligently, or at least stall until you yourself become available.

- Never sit down at your stand – potential customers feel they're disturbing you and tend to file right past without stopping.

- Take regular sit-down breaks *away* from your stand.

- Wear comfortable shoes – and an open-necked shirt if you can get away with it.

Freedom of the press belongs to the man who owns one.

A J Liebling
(quoted in Vitullo-Martin and Moskin,
1994: 182)

8

Issue a regular newsletter

It allows you to connect with clients on a regular basis and provides a useful service.

Have you every wondered what it must be like to shape public opinion? Well, wonder no more; that power is within your grasp. By writing a regular newsletter, you get to inform the segment of the public that matters most to you – your potential clients.

A readable, attractive newsletter can be devastatingly effective because it provides your target readers with information they may not have the time or inclination to go and collect themselves. In the process, it establishes your credentials as an expert in the subject matter simply because you were aware of the latest developments in your field, and brought them to their attention.

Because of the sheer pressure of work faced by most senior executives, the importance of this service that you are providing should not be underestimated. And if your newsletter is free, then you build up a substantial amount of goodwill in your personal balance sheet.

LONG OR SHORT?

Definitely short. Anything that takes longer than five minutes to read is likely to be filed (and promptly forgotten) or tossed into the bin. The people you are trying to influence are busy and already up to their neck in information; the last thing you want to do is add to their woes. 'Dying for information', a survey commissioned by Reuters in 1997, found that 48 per cent of people in the international insurance and finance sector believe that the quantity of information accumulated during the working day distracts them from their main responsibilities. Similar shock statistics apply to many other industry sectors.

WHAT TO WRITE ABOUT?

Give your readers interesting information from your area of expertise that is relevant to their business. The more objective the information, the better. It's the kind of stuff that, if your readers had the time, they would find in mainstream and technical business publications. Resist the temptation to write about your company, your expertise or your most recent sales successes – unless it's in the context of a legitimate news story. The newsletter is *not* the place for a sales pitch. Table 8.1 gives ideas for topics in a newsletter.

WHAT'S THE BEST EDITORIAL FORMAT?

Your key concern is brevity; therefore short tight, pieces are better than long, detailed ones. Here's a basic format that provides a nice mix of news and views, and is known to work very well: 5 to 10 snappy news briefs (50 to 75 words) of the kind that you normally see on the front pages of your daily newspaper; and one 'think piece' (300 to 500 words) in which you focus on a given subject as objectively as possible, quoting diverse sources for balance.

The right to be heard does not automatically include the right to be taken seriously.

Hubert H Humphrey
(quoted in Tripp, 1976: 363)

Table 8.1 *What you could be writing about*

If you're a consultant in	you could be writing about
risk management	insurance, fire, theft, lawsuits, the weather, natural disasters, executive safety, computer software, travel accidents, etc
wellness (employee well-being)	stress, diet, fitness, disease, nutrition, alternative medicine, scientific discoveries, etc
taxation	new legislation, tax rates, investment, the stock market, the economy, politics, etc

What's nice about this simple format is that it doesn't take too much time: even if you are a slow writer, you could wrap up such a newsletter in three to four hours. The news briefs are easy because, if you are reading widely in your area of expertise, you're probably collecting these titbits regularly anyway. As for the think piece, focus on any issue that you know will interest your readers. Your expertise and awareness of the deeper issues should enable you to write it fairly quickly.

WEEKLY, MONTHLY OR QUARTERLY?

Weekly is too soon; quarterly is too infrequent. Monthly is about right. Remember that time spent doing a newsletter is time spent away from your job. You're a consultant who needs to put out a newsletter from time to time, not a newsletter journalist who consults from time to time. Understand where your priorities lie and you'll get the balance right. This is all the more important as

The best copywriting advice I have ever given anybody was: write what the reader wants to read and not what the writer wants to write.

*John Frazer-Robinson
(1999)*

deadlines can be murder, and you have to get that newsletter out on time, *every* time, if it is to have any credibility. Dropping an issue is not an option.

PRINT OR ELECTRONIC?

If time and budget permit it, go for a hard-copy newsletter that can be posted to your clients. They can touch it, feel it and take it with them to a meeting – it's real. Research shows that most people prefer to read something off paper than on-screen. As a British publishing executive, Michael Lynton, has said about books – and, by extension, hard copy in general: 'The book is the greatest interactive medium of all time. You can underline it, write in the margins, fold down a page, skip ahead. And you can take it anywhere' (*The Times*, 2000).

You can achieve a good, classy feel in your newsletter without resorting to expensive paper or costly creative gimmicks. Discuss options with your design agency. For example, one way of slashing your print bill is to produce a standard template, leaving blank spaces for the stories. Run off thousands of copies of these pages, and then use them for each new edition of the newsletter until your stock runs out.

Electronic newsletters in e-mail format are definitely worth considering because they cost virtually nothing to produce (apart from your time) and can be sent to a lot of people in a matter of minutes. They are especially useful if your readership is scattered around the world.

Web site newsletters are another option: simply post your newsletter on your Web site and alert your target audience to the most recent edition by sending them an e-mail. In the early stages of my business, I found this to be the most cost-effective method of reaching the hundred most important people on my mailing list.

TO CHARGE OR NOT TO CHARGE?

What's the purpose of your newsletter? If it's to make money, then by all means charge. If, on the other hand, it's to build your public profile, then don't charge; you'll make your money through new business. Charging for an electronic newsletter is a definite no-no unless it contains proprietary information that can help your clients make money; many investment newsletters fall into this category. I must admit to having a bias towards free newsletters, because I've produced quite a few for corporate clients in my days as a corporate PR consultant and I've seen how effective they can be in bringing in new business and keeping existing clients happy.

EXAMPLES OF NEWSLETTERS

Here are three typical examples of newsletters:

- the *Pepper Report*, an e-mail newsletter;
- the *Guardrisk Update*, a hard-copy newsletter;
- the *Plain Language Update*, a Web site newsletter.

The Pepper Report

This is a short, gossip-driven online newsletter. It is written by Erich Viedge, a freelance journalist and consultant in Johannesburg (e-mail: *erich@is.co.za*; tel: 27-11 231 6470) who also teaches business executives how to deal with the media. Based to a large extent on industry gossip and the latest happenings, the *Pepper Report* has 500 regular readers in the corporate PR sector. Note the deliberately chatty tone and the clever use of low-key advertising.

It's a distressing experience and a bitter lesson for an author to find that cutting his own work improves it.

Noël Coward
(quoted in Jarski, 2000: 82)

The Pepper Report – extracts

In this issue
- Absence due to illness
- Jobs, jobs, jobs
- Kedi Segalo Award nominations

Erich's been down with tonsillitis
This issue should have hit your desks last week – but last week I had tonsillitis, believe it or not. Here I am, 31 going on 13. I emerge several kilograms lighter after 8 days flat on my back drinking water and eating soup. It's an unpleasant disease. No, I didn't have them out. My sister had hers out and still regularly gets tonsillitis.

Tony was whacked by a bus
Here's to Tony, intrepid cyclist and PR man, who was hit by a bus on the 94.7 Cycle race on Sunday. He's OK – if you can call a hairline fracture in his hip and a fractured shoulder 'OK'. Get better soon, Tony.

International scoop for Marcus Brewster!
Top publicist Marcus Brewster has contracted with British-based Marlborough Stirling to launch its South African operation in Cape Town. Over two-thirds of the UK's top 25 life companies use its systems and services as well as over half of the UK's top 25 mortgage lenders who – between them – process around 40% of British mortgages. Marcus Brewster Publicity won the business in a four-way pitch against Corporate Image, Gilmark Communications and Rosemary Hare.

――――――――――― ADVERT ―――――――――――

Looking for staff – or even a job?
Is your market the South African PR industry?
Advertise in the Pepper Report. R350 for up to six lines of text (of 80 characters each). Advertisers report excellent results.
E-mail your advert to mailto:*erich@is.co.za*

Journalists admit to grudging respect for PR pros

PR professionals rank slightly above management consultants, and are also more esteemed than lawyers, salespeople, celebrities and politicians, according to the PRWEEK/Business Wire Journalist Survey 1999. The survey polled 977 journalists across newspapers, TV, magazines and online pubs.

Work wanted

An SABC radio correspondent has just returned from Holland and is looking for work in SA. Any takers?

GBS is looking for an 'account-manager type of person'. Anybody out there?

– Do your clients consistently give journos the best possible story?
– Do your spokespeople spot a media opportunity – and exploit it every time?

Erich Viedge runs spokesperson training for up to 8 delegates. The training covers specific techniques to maximise good exposure in the press. e-mail mailto:*erich@is.co.za* or see *http://www.pepper.co.za* for more details.

Kedi Segalo Memorial Award nominees

Lisa van Leeuwen, the account executive who works on the SBIC account. Ipetla Moatse has been nominated no fewer than five times! Congratulations!

Oh, and to the Pepper Report's UK readers...

England was 122 all out in the first innings of the first test at The Wanderers. Just thought I'd let you know. Donald took 6 wickets for something like 50 runs. Pollock took 4 for 16. It's tough in Africa, wot?

Erich

Though he tortures the English language, he has never yet succeeded in forcing it to reveal its meaning.

*J B Morton
(quoted in MacHale, 1997: 51)*

The *Guardrisk Update*

This is a traditional hard-copy newsletter, yet short and snappy (see overleaf). It is issued monthly by Guardrisk, a South African risk management company, and is sent free of charge to all existing and potential clients. Within barely three years of its launch, it had become the number one must-read in the corporate risk management arena.

The Guardrisk Update

Volume 3 Issue 11   **November 1997**

SA has lost more than R18m to credit card fraud so far this year, says a Mastercard security director *(Business Day, 14 Oct)*. The loss is attributable mainly to stolen cards, which account for about 31% of all credit card-related fraud.

RANDGOLD Resources directors have started legal proceedings against BOE NatWest Securities mining analyst Barry Sergeant for alleged defamation over a draft report on the company *(Business Report, 9 Oct)*. And Guardbank is suing Martin Spring for an article in his Personal Finance newsletter calling its unit trusts "dogs" because of their poor performance over the past few years *(Financial Mail, 5 Sept)*.

ONLY 35% of SA executives exercise the medically recommended three times a week or more, and 69% of the senior workforce suffers a cholesterol problem *(Business Report, 3 Oct)*.

ABOUT 15 000 Audis have been recalled for modifications to prevent the spontaneous deployment of the airbag due to static electricity *(Business Day, 14 Oct)*. Audi says SA owners of A4, A6 and A8 models from 1995 and 1996 will be asked to take their vehicles to an Audi workshop for repairs.

A third of Gauteng's 150 reported car thefts each day are fabricated by people who succumb to the temptation of insurance fraud because they believe they will not be caught *(The Star, 8 Oct)*. An insurance industry report says vehicle-related fraud costs the industry more than R350m a year.

BECAUSE of the lack of natural catastrophes in SA history, local insurers have not felt pressured to determine their exposures accurately through modelling techniques, says Forbes Re MD Phil Pettersen *(Business Report, 21 Oct)*. The estimated insurance exposure in Gauteng alone is R520bn.

Your biggest risk may be just down the corridor

Here's a timely question for SA directors: where is one of your greatest corporate risks likely to come from within the next five years? Crime, pollution or employment practices claims? If we continue to become like the US and Europe, then the answer might well be employment practices claims. Pushing this trend are increasing democratisation of the workplace, accommodating legislation favouring employees and easier access to the courts - all of which are taking root in the new SA.

Typical claims in the US involve discrimination (race, age, sex, religion), wrongful discharge and defamation. Disability discrimination claims alone rose 1 638% from 1992 to 1995. Directors and Officers (D&O) claims show little sign of abating despite the Securities Litigation Reform Act of 1995 designed to reduce shareholder actions against directors. Even non-profit US organisations are feeling the heat: the incidence of claims has more than doubled since 1993, when only 17% of them faced such actions *(Risk Management, Sept)*. A 1996/97 Watson Wyatt Worldwide survey found that wrongful termination is the leading cause, accounting for one in four of such D&O claims.

"One of the biggest issues for risk managers in the US is how to protect companies and their directors and officers against employment practices claims," an Aon Financial Services executive told a Monte-Carlo conference. Moreover, he warned, such trends could not be ignored in Europe *(Insurance Day, 8 Oct)*.

Already, soaring claims against major UK partnerships of accountants and lawyers have prompted "dozens" of them to consider forming limited liability partnerships in the Channel Islands *("Global Focus", Business Insurance, 2 Sept)*. Price Waterhouse says a vote in favour is "a formality". A Lloyds underwriter notes: "More and more firms offering advice of any sort can expect clients to sue them." (Interestingly, there's an increasing tendency for these firms to take their corporate clients down with them when sued.) Even associations, health trusts and school bodies are now obtaining D&O coverage. The Dept. of Health estimates the cost of clinical medical claims at £156m a year and rising 25% annually. Doctors are now practising risk management.

Even in France, for years insulated against claims by tradition, law and a cosseted state sector, D&O coverage is soaring. The reasons are the internationalisation of the economy and the growing public perception that executives should be held responsible for their actions.

What can companies do in a showdown with employees or clients? Mediate rather than litigate, suggests local attorney Steven Nackan *(Business Day, 9 Oct)*. It allows disputes to be solved in days, if not hours. He says 850 US corporations and 3200 other companies have signed pacts to use mediation as a first recourse to resolving disputes. Success rates are around 85% to 90%. Another example of Churchill's saying that jaw, jaw is better than war, war?

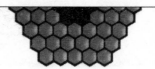

Risk barometer

GERMAN insurer HDI has launched a product recall insurance policy which covers costs incurred through ordinary recalls and extortion - a common problem in the food industry *(Insurance Day, 7 Oct)*. It also includes losses from reduced sales. In 1993, snack producer Bahlsen suffered reduced sales of over $29m from its paprika chips recall.

A New York appellate court has upheld a lower court decision that a business cannot be sued in a state just because it has an Internet site that can be accessed by residents of that state *(Business Insurance, 22 Sept)*. The judges nevertheless said that "attempting to apply established trademark law in the fast-developing world of the Internet is like trying to board a moving bus".

OFFICIALS from the New York Metropolitan Transportation Authority are studying the possibility of forming a New York-domiciled captive which could be the first to be formed under the state's recently approved captive law *(Business Insurance, 15 Sept)*. The law, which takes effect on 5 December, allows large public authorities to form captives in the state.

MAN-MADE disasters - including industrial and transport accidents - made up 54% of total disasters between 1971 and 1996, according to the World Disasters Report issued by the Red Cross *(The Economist, 6 Sept)*.

COMPANY failures in Europe have doubled over the past ten years, from 100 000 to 200 000, yet most companies do not have credit insurance *(Insurance Day, 8 Oct)*.

EUROPEAN managers have overestimated their preparedness for both the Millennium bomb (the "Y2K problem") and the impending changeover from local currencies to the Euro, which is set to start in 1998 *(Insurance Day, 9 Oct)*. That's according to two reports from London-based consultants Neaman Bond Associates.

Never trust anyone you don't understand.

Jack Trout with Steve Rivkin
(1999: 40)

The *Plain Language Update*

This was a Web site-based newsletter consisting of short news items that I used to produce in the early stages of my consultancy. The news items were posted on my Web site and clients would be informed of new editions via e-mail. Note the links to Gobbledygook Corner, a popular part of the Web site.

The Plain Language Update – extracts

SA parliament to learn plain English

South Africa's parliament is cracking down on the use of legalistic, convoluted language. Dr Frene Ginwala, Speaker of Parliament, said in a radio interview that Parliament would be introducing lectures and training programmes for both MPs and staff. 'The language [used] is very, very legalistic,' she said. 'Nobody understands half the things that are said. They use fifty words when they could use one.'

  Radio interview on SAFm, 15 July 98

'Synergy' gets more bad press

The word 'synergy', which is frequently used (incorrectly) by companies to describe the benefits of a merger, has been criticized yet again – this time by William Lutz, a professor at Rutgers University in the US. Lutz, who has played a key role in the Securities and Exchange Commission's plain language programme, says the word has become so overused that it no longer has any meaning. Quoted in the on-line edition of *The Record* (21 January), he says: 'These guys don't have the faintest idea of what a synergy is, and they wouldn't know it if it ran them down in the street... Take me by the hand and lead me to a synergy.'

New book out on keeping it simple

Marketing guru Jack Trout's new book, *The Power of Simplicity* (McGraw-Hill), is sure to find favour with plain language fans. Described as 'a management guide to cutting through the nonsense and doing things right', it encourages clarity and simplicity in everything from language to strategic planning. Two quotes worth remembering: 'Never trust anyone you don't understand' and 'Big ideas almost always come in small words'.

NASA employee rewrites safety manual

US vice-president Al Gore has awarded Den Clem, a NASA employee, his monthly Plain Language Award for his key role in rewriting a NASA safety manual. The 600-plus page Safety and Health Handbook was rewritten in plain language using a user-friendly question-and-answer format. See Gobble-dygook Corner on this website for an extract from the rewritten manual.
From US Newswire, 20 July 1999

Shareholder documents under fire

South African shareholder documents (prospectuses, circulars, schemes of arrangement, etc) are way over the head of the average shareholder and should be made more user-friendly. That's the majority view of a group of 24 lawyers, stockbrokers, investment analysts, individual shareholders, financial journalists and stock exchange officials. They were polled by Markinor, the research organisation, in a study commissioned by Rand Merchant Bank and Plain Business Writing. If you'd like a free copy of this interesting report, send an e-mail to *maureen.gleeson@rmb.co.za* at Rand Merchant Bank, or *query@plainwriting.co.za* at Plain Business Writing. Please don't forget to include your postal address.

BBC dumps Latin title of famous TV series

The BBC has renamed *QED*, its 18-year-old, award-winning science series, because viewers 'didn't have the faintest idea what QED meant'. Following research that uncovered a distinctly shaky grasp of Latin among television audiences, BBC1 has given the series the more straightforward title *Living Proof*. QED is an abbreviation of the Latin phrase *quod erat demonstrandum*, which means 'what had to be demonstrated'. (One reader of a British newspaper, tongue no doubt firmly in cheek, wrote that he had always thought QED meant 'Quite Easily Done'.)
From the Weekly Telegraph, 29 Sept to 5 Oct 1999

249 documents to process one arrest

It took a UK policeman his entire nine-hour shift and a staggering 249 pieces of paperwork to process one simple arrest. PC Richard Thomas embarked on his form-filling marathon after being called in to arrest a 19-year-old who had been stopped allegedly trying to steal a bottle of whisky from a supermarket. Ian Westwood, vice-chairman of the Police Federation, called it a massive waste of time. 'We invent forms for every scenario,' he said. 'When I first joined the force 29 years ago, an entire traffic incident could be dealt with on one piece of paper.'
From UK Mail, 30 August 1999

*You cannot <u>bore</u> people into buying your product.
You can only <u>interest</u> them in buying it.*

*David Ogilvy
(1983: 80)*

9

Advertise – but do so intelligently

Go for small, cost-effective ads. Send brochures, flyers and e-mail to your target market.

There's something about advertising that gets us all abuzz with excitement. The first thing we want to do when we've started a new business is draw up a big, colourful advertisement and stick it in a prominent business publication. We're absolutely convinced everyone will see it. After all, it's so *big*!

Welcome to the urge to advertise. Problem is, advertising seduces by its visibility (look, there's my ad!) yet disappoints by its lack of results. Many consultants will learn this the hard way – I certainly did. Unless your ads are running on a regular basis, you'll find that they produce a bad return on investment. They are expensive to produce and equally expensive to flight, whether in newspapers, on radio or on TV.

Advertising is useful when you want to establish your brand in a largely anonymous marketplace where you don't personally know the people buying your product. That's why manufacturers of washing powder or baked beans splash out so heavily on advertising; it helps them to distinguish their product from those of the competition, and creates a brand personality that people can relate to.

Consultancy, however, is not a mass-market product. You bill by the hour, which means you're selling time. How do you brand time? What lifestyle message do you attach to it? Also, you know exactly who your potential buyers are. Assuming you haven't already built up a database of prospects by virtue of your years of experience, you could easily build one by spending a few days on the phone, or consulting one of the numerous corporate directories on sale in major bookshops.

For these two reasons – you sell a service and you know who you sell it to – traditional advertising is not always the best way to go. Rather, take the tools of traditional advertising and adapt them to your situation. Here are some techniques that will produce results if you have the budget.

EXPERIMENT WITH SMALL, AFFORDABLE ADS

Large expensive ads won't work, but small ones might. Take out the smallest ad possible in major business publications or mainstream newspapers. Matchbox-size ads are a good bet, especially if they have a catchy colour. Keep the message extremely short, and advertise just one aspect of your service. For example, if you're an IT consultant and you issue a free newsletter, your ad might contain the words 'Free IT newsletter' followed by a contact number. If you have a really catchy Web site address that unambiguously conveys what you do, then run just that in your ad, for example *www.hot-investment-tips.com.*

INSERT YOUR BROCHURE INTO MAJOR MAGAZINES

An insert is simply a brochure or pamphlet that is inserted into a business publication – more often a magazine than a newspaper.

It doesn't take a rocket scientist to know that <u>the most critical element in an ad is the headline</u>. If the headline doesn't work, the game is over.

George Duncan
(2001)

Inserts are particularly useful when your message is a long one. For example, if you were running a workshop or training course, an insert would give you the space in which to cover the content, pricing and booking procedure. To increase the likelihood that readers will notice your material as they read the magazine, insist that your brochure be dropped in *all on its own* on a given page, even if you have to pay the magazine an additional fee for the privilege. Otherwise, it ends up with everyone else's material, and you get lost in the clutter. (It's a source of amazement that magazines don't automatically provide this service, given the large number of inserts many of them stuff into each issue.)

SEND YOUR BROCHURE DIRECTLY TO YOUR TARGET COMPANIES

Since you have a list of your target companies as well as the key contact people, why not just send them your brochure, accompanied by a short covering letter? This is what's known as a mailshot. However, envelopes and postage can be costly, especially if you have a large target audience. Also, the covering letters can be time-consuming: although they don't have to be done one at a time thanks to the mail merge facility on your computer, you still have to sign every single one of them by hand.

CONTACT COMPANIES BY E-MAIL

First we had mailshots; now we have e-mail shots. This involves obtaining the e-mail address of your key contacts, and then sending them a brief – repeat, brief – message emphasizing one particular aspect of your service. The trick is to make your message so short that the start and end are visible on screen without the need to scroll. For example, if you're a training consultant pushing the need

My rule of pinkie today is to estimate 1% response, and if the numbers don't work at that response rate, re-think the project.

George Duncan
(2001)

for increased productivity, and you've just written an interesting report on the subject, your e-mail might read:

Dear Bill

We've just released an interesting research report entitled MOST STAFF CAN'T TYPE – AND IT'S COSTING COMPANIES MILLIONS.

The report is free. To order, go to our Web site www.HR-productivity.com and click on FREE REPORT on the home page.

Thanks!

John Smith
CEO: HR Productivity.

Note the sly way you force Bill to visit your Web site and learn more about your company. In fact, as part of the process of ordering, you might even include the option 'Click here if you'd like to receive future reports'. That way, you get Bill on to your database with his consent.

KEEP YOUR BROCHURES SIMPLE

Most promotional brochures are notoriously ineffective because they have been designed to look pretty rather than to be read. With their zany colours, unreadable fonts, bad layout and lack of white space, they are a triumph of style over functionality. When you sit down with your design agency, insist on a functional brochure. It's a sad fact, confirmed by experience and countless research studies, that an embarrassingly large number of design agencies the world over are singularly incapable of designing for readability. As former Australian newspaperman Colin Wheildon says in his aptly titled report 'Communicating – or just making pretty shapes' (Newspaper Advertising Bureau of Australia): 'A design that looks exciting but is incomprehensible is nothing more than a beautifully painted square wheel... Good design is a balance between function and form, and the greater of these is function.'

BE PREPARED FOR LOW RESPONSE RATES

Here's something that might shock you unless you've been exposed to the world of marketing and advertising: response rates – the rate at which people respond to your advertisement, brochure or mailshot – are notoriously low. The main reason is that people don't consciously open a publication with the express intention of reading your insert; they want to read the articles. As for your mailshot, it is essentially unsolicited mail that ends up competing with other more important mail on your reader's desk. That's why advertising has been defined as the art of arresting the intelligence sufficiently long to get money out of it. A response rate of 1 to 2 per cent is about average, which means that out of 100 people who actually see your material, only one or two will respond. A response rate of 5 to 10 per cent is truly excellent. If you get that on a sustained basis, write a book about it because you'll have discovered the holy grail! The most important factors affecting your response rate are:

- the ease with which your message can be digested at a glance;
- the timing of your message;
- the readership profile of the publication.

In general, you can expect a good response rate if your message is easy to grasp, goes off at the right time and is targeted at the right level of person in the organization.

Copy should be written in the language people use in everyday conversation, as in this anonymous verse:

Carnation Milk is the best in the land,
Here I sit with a can in my hand
No tits to pull, no hay to pitch
Just punch a hole in the son-of-a-bitch.

David Ogilvy
(1983: 81)

EXAMPLES OF BROCHURES

The following pages show what good, effective brochures look like. Note the utter simplicity of the design, and the heavy use of bold, easy-to-catch headlines:

- At last – legal contracts in plain language…
- Tired of longwinded writing?
- 3 steps to better business writing.

Brochure 1: DL size, 4 sides

Reading time *25 minutes*
Book length *64 pages*

Price *R85 plus VAT*

If you're one of those lawyers who has always longed to write clear, simple legal contracts but never quite dared to, then this book is for you.

It applies proven, common-sense principles of clarity and brevity to leases, insurance policies and related contracts in order to make them more readable.

The myth that contracts are necessarily unreadable because the subject matter is complex is neatly demolished. Through the use of before/after examples and real-world case studies, you'll see for yourself that a contract can be legally precise and easy to understand.

In this booklet, you'll learn to:

- write every single clause in plain language
- use headlines, summaries and a clean layout
- minimise definitions, cross-referencing and other irritations.

To order

Orders by fax, e-mail or website only:

NOTE! new contact numbers

tel: (011) 881-5570

fax: (011) 881-5504

e-mail: *query@plainwriting.co.za*

website: *www.plainwriting.co.za*

Other booklets in the series

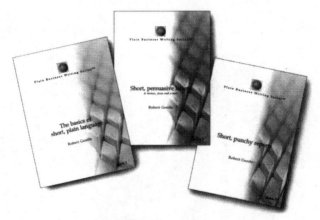

Reading time *20 minutes*

Price *R50 each plus VAT*

Plain Business Writing Series™

Tired of longwinded writing?

Brochure 2: A4 size, leaflet, 2 sides

Visit our stand at:

Human Resources Africa 2000
Gallagher Estate, Midrand
7 – 9 June

tel: (011) 881-5570 **fax:** (011) 881-5504
e-mail: *query@plainwriting.co.za*
website: *www.plainwriting.co.za*

Plain Business Writing

In use at over **800** companies

3 steps to better **business writing**

Brochure 3: A5 size, 2-fold, 6 sides

step 1

Learn the basics

Learn to grab and sustain your reader's attention by mastering the fundamentals:

- plain words
- short sentences
- point up-front
- descriptive headlines
- clean, airy layout.

Reading time *20 minutes*
Price *R50 plus VAT*

step**2**   **Practise the basics**

Come see a demo
We do regular big-screen demonstrations at our offices. Call (011) 881-5570 for a booking.

How it works
This 90-minute computer-based training course
features author Robert Gentle on video as well as numerous examples and exercises. It can be loaded onto your desktop, laptop or company network.

step**3**

Apply the basics

Reading time *20 minutes*
Price *R50 plus VAT*

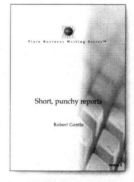

Reading time *20 minutes*
Price *R50 plus VAT*

Reading time *25 minutes*
Price *R85 plus VAT*

Reading time *25 minutes*
Price *R110 plus VAT*

An easy-to-read format

Prices

For orders of 3000 copies or more per book, we can do a special, **customised print run** in your own corporate colours.

Books	Basics	R50
	Letters	R50
	Reports	R50
	Contracts	R85
	Annual reports	R110

discounts of 10% to 25% for orders of 100 copies or more per book

CD-ROM	**Cost of a user license**	
	Small companies	R10 000
	Medium-sized companies	R25 000
	Large companies	R50 000

To order

fax (011) 881-5504   **e-mail** *query@plainwriting.co.za*
web *www.plainwriting.co.za*   **queries** tel: (011) 881-5570

All prices exclude VAT.

Plain Business Writing Series™

I love it when a plan comes together!

> *Colonel John 'Hannibal' Smith*
> *[this was usually the last line of each episode]*
> *(From The A-Team, 1983–88*
> *produced by Universal TV)*

10

Pulling it all together

Avoid marketing by the seat of your pants; rather go for marketing techniques that suit strategic objectives.

The best marketing ideas come not at random, but as solutions to particular problems – or, put another way, as a means of achieving certain objectives. Therefore, your challenge is to define your consultancy business in terms of strategic objectives, and then see what ways and means suggest themselves.

When I started my plain-language consultancy, I knew that I wanted to consult to companies, rewrite complex documentation in plain language and train their staff in the techniques of good writing. That was the easy part. The marketing challenge was to make the corporate sector see my services as not just desirable, but indispensable. I sat down with a felt-tipped pen and a piece of A3 paper and sketched the following broad strategy for the first full year of operation:

- **Publicize plain English** – *create awareness*.
  - Issue reports.
  - Write media articles.

- Speak at conferences.
- Speak at companies.
- Issue a guide to plain English.
- **Get the authorities onside** – *create respectability*.
  - Meet with the Financial Services Board.
  - Meet with the Stock Exchange.
  - Meet with the Consumer Council.
  - Meet with the Institute of Directors.
  - Meet with the Banking Council, etc.
- **Establish standards** – *create pressure to conform*.
  - Create a certification mark.
  - Have an annual award for good, clear writing in financial services.
  - Have an annual award for bad writing across all industries.

Once key objectives were clearly listed, solutions progressively suggested themselves. Some were easier than others. For example, creating awareness led to fairly obvious things such as press coverage, briefings and speaking at conferences. But how to establish standards was trickier. One solution that ended up working very well was an annual competition for financial services companies, my key target market. It was done in conjunction with *Personal Finance*, a leading weekly publication that is required reading by the financial services sector.

The following year, with these objectives largely met, the strategy evolved to include the training of corporate staff. That pushed me into exhibiting my training material at trade exhibitions, and redesigning my Web site to allow for online selling.

WHAT ARE YOUR STRATEGIC OBJECTIVES?

If you're about to start a consultancy, draw up a list of strategic objectives and then see which specific marketing techniques meet

It isn't that they can't see the solution. It is that they can't see the problem.

G K Chesterton
(quoted in Ratcliffe, 2000)

those objectives. If you've already been operating for a while, draw up a list anyway to see where your business is heading; then check if your existing marketing effort corresponds with those objectives. For example, you might be plugging away trying to get lots of press coverage, which certainly doesn't hurt; but if your real objective is to reach potential clients and educate them about your particular area of expertise, then newsletters and reports would be far more effective.

FROM THEORY TO PRACTICE

Example 1

You're an expert in industrial safety, and know that government is about to pass new legislation compelling companies to raise their safety standards at great cost. Let's assume that this level of safety is fairly new internationally, and exists only in Switzerland, Sweden and a handful of states in the USA. You want to become a consultant advising local industrial companies on how to comply with the new legislation and how best to implement it on the shop floor. Here's what your strategic objectives might be, and the corresponding marketing techniques you could consider employing:

- **Become an industry expert.**
  - Do lots of research (books, reports).
  - Surf the Internet.
  - Visit relevant companies in Switzerland, Sweden and the USA.
- **Educate government and industry.**
  - Write a report based on the trip to Switzerland, Sweden and the United States.
  - Make copies available to government legislators and do presentations.
  - Make copies available to companies and do presentations.
- **Educate the media.**
  - Hold a media conference on the trip to Switzerland, Sweden and the United States.

- Make copies of the report available to the press, radio and TV.
- Be available for journalists who want quotes for their stories.

Of course, things won't necessarily end here. If, for example, you extended an invitation to two of the experts you met overseas to visit your country and speak about the implementation of the new safety standards, you may want to add 'Organize a conference' to your 'Educate the market' strategy. These experts could then become the keynote speakers at the conference.

Two years down the line, you may have developed such a high level of expertise on the subject that you could easily write a book about it.

Example 2

You're a stress management expert who has just designed a two-day workshop aimed at the corporate sector. However, your research suggests that most companies are either hostile or indifferent to the subject, and regard it as being somewhat wishy-washy and outside the mainstream. Here's how you might go about breaking down this attitude and making the market more receptive:

- **Educate the corporate market.**
    - Write a pocket-sized 'Quick Stress Test' guide, print thousands of copies and mail it to the corporate sector. Make sure it lands on the right desks (eg human resources heads, company doctors or psychologists).
    - Write a regular column on corporate stress management, post it on your Web site and alert your target market by e-mail. Try and get a newspaper to run the column too.
    - Write an annual report each year that covers developments in stress management in the corporate sector, publicize it in the media and mail it into the corporate market free of charge.

It is a bad plan that admits of no modification.

Publilius Syrus
(quoted in Kipfer, 1994)

- **Educate the public and the media.**
  - Write letters to the editor on stress-related issues, making sure they tie in to topical developments.
  - Write articles on stress management issues.
  - Cultivate the media and nurture contacts so that journalists always quote you in their articles on stress-related issues.
- **Market your workshop.**
  - Place small, cost-effective advertisements in the right publications.
  - Send out flyers and brochures to your target market.
  - Go into companies and do free, introductory lectures on stress management; this should whet their appetite for the full workshop.

Again, things would not end here, and you'd need to be alert to sudden opportunities. For example, you'd almost certainly end up being invited to speak at conferences because of your high public profile. Better still, proactively seek out conferences at which you'd like to speak, and get yourself invited. You might even want to co-organize and co-sponsor your own national conference.

EVERYTHING INFLUENCES EVERYTHING ELSE

As explained in the very first chapter of this book, a good marketing programme creates a virtuous circle in which your various marketing activities reinforce one another. Thus your press coverage increases your visibility at networking functions; your networking helps you to land new business; your new business adds to your knowledge; your increased knowledge allows you to write more articles in the press – and so on. The whole is greater than the sum of the parts.

Marketplace results are the function of both strategy and implementation. Just as ineffective implementation undermines an effective strategy, skilled implementation of a weak or inappropriate strategy wastes resources.

Kevin J Clancy and Peter C Krieg
(2000)

WHERE TO FROM HERE?

As with all things in life, success comes from doing a few things well – and this short book contains the few things you need to market yourself effectively. You could start as early as tomorrow. The trick is to get rolling and maintain the momentum. It won't take long for the results to start showing. One fine day, weeks or months from now, you'll get a phone call out of the blue from a potential client who has heard of you somewhere – that's when you'll know your marketing effort is starting to bear fruit. Good luck!

Well-found consultants can stay in a company forever, moving from one divisional troublespot to another like Arabs wandering from oasis to oasis.

Robert Heller
(quoted in Crainer, 1997)

References

Associated Press (2001) *Associated Press Broadcast News Handbook: A manual of techniques and practices*, McGraw-Hill, New York

BBC (1998) *Sorry, I Haven't a Clue*, Orion Books, London

Buckley, Reid (1999) *Strictly Speaking*, McGraw-Hill, New York

Clancy, Kevin J and Krieg, Peter C (2000) *Counter-intuitive Marketing*, The Free Press, New York

Crainer, Stuart (1997) *The Ultimate Book of Business Quotations*, Capstone Publishing, Oxford

Duncan, George (2001) *Direct Marketing: How to use the Internet, direct mail and other media to generate direct sales*, Adams Media Corporation, Holbrook, MA

Ehrlich, Henry (1998) *The Wiley Book of Business Quotations*, John Wiley & Sons, New York

Forbes Inc (1997) *The Forbes Book of Quotations*, Black Dog & Leventhal, New York

Frazer-Robinson, John (1999) *Effective Direct Mail*, David Grant Publishing, Pembury, Kent

Gentle, Robert (2001) *Read This: Business writing that works*, Pearson Education, London

Glover, Stephen, ed (1999) *The Penguin Book of Journalism: Secrets of the press*, Penguin, London

Jarski, Rosemarie (2000) *Hollywood Wit*, Prion Books, London

Kipfer, Barbara Ann, comp (1994) *Bartlett's Book of Business Quotations*, Little, Brown & Company, Boston

Lamb, G F (2000) *Apt and Amusing Quotations*, Elliot Right Way Books, Tadworth, Surrey

MacHale, Des (1996) *Wit*, Prion Books, London

MacHale, Des (1997) *More Wit*, Prion Books, London

Metcalf, Fred, comp (1986) *The Penguin Dictionary of Modern Humorous Quotations*, Penguin, London

Ogilvy, David (1983) *Ogilvy on Advertising*, Prion Books, London

Ratcliffe, S, ed (2000) *The Oxford Dictionary of Thematic Quotations*, Oxford University Press, Oxford

Ries, Al and Ries, Laura (1998) *The 22 Immutable Laws of Branding*, HarperCollins Business, London

Russell, J Thomas and Lane, W Ronald (1998) *Kleppner's Advertising Procedure*, 14th edn, Prentice-Hall, Upper Saddle River, NJ

The Times (2000) *The Times Book of Quotations*, HarperCollins Publishers, London

Tripp, R T, comp (1976) *The International Thesaurus of Quotations*, Penguin, London

Trout, Jack (2000) *Differentiate or Die: Survival in our era of killer competition*, John Wiley & Sons, New York

Trout, Jack with Rivkin, Steve (1999) *The Power of Simplicity*, McGraw-Hill, New York

Vitullo-Martin, Julia and Moskin, J Robert (1994) *Executive's Book of Quotations*, Oxford University Press, New York

Woods, John (2000) *The Quotable Executive*, McGraw-Hill, New York

Index